JESUS
Man of Joy

SHERWOOD E. WIRT

HARVEST HOUSE PUBLISHERS
Eugene, Oregon 97402

Jesus, Man of Joy
Copyright © 1999 by Sherwood Eliot Wirt
Published by Harvest House Publishers
Eugene, Oregon 97402

Library of Congress Cataloging-in-Publication Data

Wirt, Sherwood Eliot.
  Jesus, man of joy / Sherwood E. Wirt.
    p. cm.
  ISBN 0-7369-0046-2
  1. Joy—Religious aspects—Christianity.
  2. Jesus Christ—Character.   I. Title.
BV4647.J68W58   1999
232.9'03—dc21   98-31333
                                    CIP

Printed in the United States of America.

99 00 01 02 / BP / 10 9 8 7 6 5 4

To

Bob and Jennie Gillespie

These words I have spoken to you
that My joy may remain in you,
and that your joy may be full.

—JOHN 15:11

Acknowledgment

What a pleasure to write this book! It has been like strolling through an archway of rainbows. Fascinating things happen to people when they start looking for joy in God's Word, for the joy appears in such varied and colorful ways. The Holy Spirit shows Himself as more than a Comforter; He becomes an Encourager and Inspirer who fills ordinary lives with moments of divine bliss.

This book came to be through the kind help of friends who are excellent writers themselves. Many of them are active members of the San Diego County Christian Writers' Guild. In particular I would mention Nancy Bayless, Judith Dupree, Kathryn Hughes, Jean Mader, Elaine Minton, Glenda Palmer, Judith Scharfenburg, Candace Walters, and Claudia Ward. My nonpareil critic is, as usual, my wife, Ruth Love Wirt, who sent many of my purple passages tumbling over the Sunset Cliffs.

Seeing this manuscript through the press has been a genuine pleasure. The founder of Harvest House, Robert Hawkins, Sr., is an old friend and a Christian gentleman with a warm heart for writers. My thanks go to him and all the active personnel of Harvest House for their professional labors on this work. I would especially mention Jerry MacGregor, senior editor; Robert Hawkins, Jr., publisher; Carolyn McCready, editorial director; and Ray Oehm, editor. Also I would include Bruce Marchiano, actor, author, preacher, and good friend, for a whole bushel of kindnesses.

A prominent European theologian once commented that "orthodoxy has no humor." Anyone who thinks this way should subscribe without delay to "The Joyful Noiseletter," published by my friend Cal Samra, founder of the Fellowship of Merry Christians, at Box 895, Portage, MI 49081. Mr. Samra has given percipient support to the writing of this book, for which I am grateful.

Contents

FOREWORD

"Bruce, I have one word for you: JOY!"

THESE WERE THE WORDS SPOKEN to me by film director Regardt van den Bergh over lunch in December 1992. He had asked me, an actor, to play the role of Jesus in *The Visual Bible: The Gospel of Matthew*, and this was the sum total of his direction—joy.

I will never forget it as long as I live. He whipped a dog-eared Bible out of his rear pocket, cracked it open to Hebrews 1:9, and read straight from the Scriptures: "Therefore God, Your God, has set You above Your companions by anointing you with the *oil of joy*." Then he looked me in the eye with all the conviction of a man who would bet everything he owns on something he knows beyond knowing and proclaimed, "Bruce, I've prayed and prayed about this, and I'm convinced this is what the Lord would have us do in *Matthew*: to portray Jesus as a *man of joy*."

I remember staring blankly across the table at Regardt that afternoon, cautiously nodding. I had no idea at the time, but his words would rewrite completely my understanding of my Savior and liberate me into a level of relationship with Him I never dreamed possible. And what's more, those same words expressed on film many months later would liberate untold thousands across the planet into a level of relationship with the Savior *they* never dreamed possible. And all of it stemmed from what could very well be the most obvious, most overlooked, most disregarded, most neglected, most misunderstood, most undefined,

9

most manipulated left-behind, swept-under-the-carpet-and-barred-from-hallowed-church-halls reality in all of Christendom: that Jesus was a man of joy.

"But, Bruce, what's the big deal? So Jesus laughed. So Jesus smiled. So what if He was a nice guy to be around. After all, I've got premillennial dispensationalism to think about, and then there's the 10–40 window, and choir practice, and that home-schooling seminar. And besides, God is serious business, and what have wrath and judgment got to do with joy and smiling and stuff like that? Stuff that's, well, frankly, *for kids*." And I think Jesus might reply: "Have you never read, 'from the lips of *children* and infants you have ordained praise'? And unless you change and become like little *children*, you will never enter the kingdom of heaven. Therefore whosoever humbles himself like a *child* is the greatest in the kingdom of heaven . . . *for the kingdom of heaven belongs to such as these.*"[1]

May I read to you from a letter I received about a year ago?

> Please bear with my penmanship, as my hands have become stiff with age and arthritis. I have loved the Lord as my Savior for many years—ever since I was a teenager. I always thought I knew who He was. In fact, I never once questioned who He was (is). But a few weeks ago I was halfway watching TV and happened to look up and there was "Jesus" (you) walking along the banks of the Sea of Galilee with the wind blowing His robes and hair. He slowly looked over His shoulder, smiled a big smile, and motioned to follow Him. My heart leaped right out of my chest! Even though it was only a two-second glimpse, I couldn't believe my eyes. It was Jesus like I'd never considered Him to be, and in a moment I was convinced in my heart that Jesus just had to be this way—completely different from everything I'd ever thought! Glowing with excitement from His face—from His eyes. A strong, energetic, passionate, joyous man! It instantaneously transformed my relationship with Him—so much so, I grieve to think of all the decades I've wasted knowing Him, but not *knowing* Him; loving Him and receiving His love from some distant place, but never being

"in love" with Him. Well, I want you to know that I am now! I've thrown out every picture of a stale Jesus I ever owned. Martha is out, and Mary is in. I've stopped cowering before my Lord and started celebrating Him! All the old people at the home here think I've gone crazy, but I feel that I'm sane for the very first time in my life! Oh the Joy! My Jesus, my Lord!

Christian, I know you walk with the Lord, but in all humility I ask, "Do you know Him? Do you *really, really* know who He *really, really* is?" Non-Christian, I know as of this reading you're not all that interested in Jesus, at least to the point of inviting Him into your life as Lord and Savior. But in all humility, I ask, "Do you know? Do you *really, really* know?"

In the pages that follow, Sherwood (but you can call me "Woody") Wirt, has the privilege of unveiling the reality of Jesus Christ of Nazareth in all the explosive joy that being the Son of the Living God "made man" had to be. It is an absolute treasure, this reality, this joy—a treasure of life-transforming value that, sadly, has been lying at our feet almost completely overlooked for far too long.

I have read some of the pages that follow countless times. I have carried them with me on countless airplanes and into hotel rooms across this country and the world. I had a well-marked copy sitting on my dresser in Morocco every day of the *Matthew* film shoot and in South Africa every day of my six months of ministry that followed. I even have an original copy sitting on my coffee table right now and a still-in-the-plastic spare tucked safely into a cupboard, just in case.

You see, as I ramble through the busyness of life, career, and ministry, there is one thing I must always be keenly aware of: who Jesus *really* is. That reality is an absolute treasure, and it is a treasure contained in this book, *Jesus, Man of Joy*.

So rejoice and be glad! It's a gloriously new day! And whether you've walked with Jesus for a hundred years or never at all, *open your heart* that through the pages that follow you might possibly meet Him in a brand-new way.

Come! And as the Letter to the Hebrews proclaims, "Let us fix our eyes on Jesus!" Let us sit at His feet; let us hear His heart and feel His embrace; let us gaze into His smile, hear His laughter, touch the hem of His garment, and be liberated into His joy! Ultimate joy! The joy of Jesus!

—Bruce Marchiano

The Phone Rang

"Hello."

"Hello; Mr. Wirt?"

"Yes."

"My name is Bruce Marchiano. I'm an actor and a friend of Teres Byrne."

"Teres! Where is she?"

"Here in Hollywood."

"She's funny, that one. I'd say she's the best comedienne since Fanny Brice. How is she?"

"Oh, she's fine. Busy. Mr. Wirt, I'm calling about your little paperback book, *Jesus, Man of Joy*."[1]

"Join the crowd. They're all calling me from everywhere wanting a copy, but I'm sorry to tell you it's dead. I'm down to one copy."

"It's not dead, sir. It's a terrific book. It helped me fill the role of Jesus in our new motion picture, *The Gospel According to Matthew*."

"What?"

"I'm telling you, when I found that book it was a treasure trove. Jesus began jumping off the page at me. Joy! Exactly what I needed. And I took it to Morocco to begin shooting."

"Did you say your name was Bruce?"

"Yes, sir."

"And you're a Hollywood actor?"

"Yes."

"Well, may the saints be glorified! And you took that book of mine to Morocco?"

"I sure did. I copied it out, memorized parts of it, and carried it everywhere."

"Bruce, that little tome has been embalmed and buried six feet deep for the last two years. You might honor it with a moment of silence."

"No, sir, it's due for a resurrection. I'm sending you four video-cassettes of *The Gospel According to Matthew*.[2] And I'm sending with them my new book, *In the Footsteps of Jesus*. It tells about you and your book and how it helped me."[3]

"What did you say about it?"

"I said every page of your book was loaded with gems. I said I couldn't highlight phrases or scribble notes fast enough. It was the guide I'd been hunting for. Since the night I found it, I've read it over and over, cover to cover."

"In what field did you find this treasure trove that filled you with all that joy so you bought the field?"

"In a Glendale bookstore, the day before we left L.A. It was hidden behind another book and turned out to be just what I was looking for. The director told me he wanted to portray Jesus as joy-ful. I kept looking and looking for a book like that, and yours turned out to be it."

"Flabbergasting. That's what it is. Mind-boggling."

"Can I tell you a story about Jesus and His joy?"

"Okay."

"It seems Teres is a kind of honorary aunt to three kids in her church she calls 'The Bunny, The Buddy, and the Budley.' Well, Teres told these kids that she knew me, and that I was going to play Jesus in a new movie. So then the 'Bunny,' Monica Farrar, eight years old, spoke up and said, 'Well, I sure hope He *smiles* a lot, because in the other movies Jesus never smiled, and I know that Jesus smiles all the time!'"

"Right on! I'd like that in my own book."

"I told Teres that little Monica lit fireworks in my heart. Wait till you see the film. It's all taken right out of the Gospel of Matthew. My only words are the words of Jesus."

"Mr. Marchiano—Bruce—thanks. You've set off some fire-works in my own heart. God bless you."

—S.E.W.

Stirrings in Heaven

ONE

An Astonishing Change

*In joy something goes out from
oneself to the universe.*
—RICHARD HOOKER

TWO THOUSAND YEARS AGO THERE appeared on this planet
a Person who brought about an astonishing change in the quality of life among human beings. Whatever this Person had, it
was unique. It set Him apart and made Him utterly fascinating
to others. For a few brief years He appeared in the villages and
towns of Palestine, which at the time were under Roman occu-
pation. Then He disappeared, although some of His close followers claimed they had reason to believe He was—and is—still
around.

Remarkable actions were attributed to Him, but He wrote
no epics and raised no monuments. In early youth He seems to
have worked with His hands. Later He taught, prayed, and
healed, as many prophets had done before Him and have done
since then. That He had noble character and personal charm,
and uttered many wise things that people have been saying ever
since, could be said also of others.

Yet for this Person to be endowed with such universal
appeal required something very special to attach to Him. The
world has never forgotten Him. His name is on someone's lips

every second of time; in fact, time is dated from His birth. A billion human beings today claim to be His followers, and most of them are convinced that He is the Author of their personal salvation.

But if there was "something special" about Him, in what did it consist? Gilbert Chesterton tells us that He had a secret. But what secret? I believe you may find it in the pages that follow. It has been divulged before, but still many people appear not to have found it. Even among some of those who have risen to high eminence in His service, it is still, tragically, a secret. Some people are known to live earnest and godly lives. They perform wonderful deeds and achieve mighty goals that bring abundant blessings to the human race. It seems inexplicable that they should miss the secret, but the fact is that they do.

What makes this all so strange is that it is an open secret, spread throughout the New Testament for everyone to read. It may not be spelled out on every page, for a very good reason; and yet its effect can be felt all through the 27 books and letters. It is a secret that explains, more than anything else, the grip that this Person has held upon the lives of ordinary mankind and womankind for these two millennia. It also helps to explain what God had in mind when He created the universe and placed humans in it.

Millions of human beings today are going through a very hard time. They know something is wrong. Instinct tells them there is something better for them than what they are having to put up with, but they seem helpless to attain it.

> Thou madest man, he knows not why,
> He thinks he was not made to die.[1]

Lily Tomlin, the television comedienne who rose to television fame through her unforgettable portrayals in "Laugh-in," made this statement in an interview that appeared in the *San Francisco Chronicle*: "In a world where so many things are brutalizing and desensitizing, maybe we yearn to make something that fills us with a kind of elation, a sense of something joyful or lovely, a sense of inspiration. Anything to make us rise above this banal, animalistic, low-grade, diminished, cockroach level."[2]

I do not pretend to possess any special credentials or qualifications for this effort to "make something." But of what use are credentials when one is writing about the mind of the One who operates the cosmos? You may be certain that I have discovered nothing new. The secret has been there all the time, and while some people have found it, many others haven't.

Back in 1870 a young American sailed to England with that secret. One person who heard him preach said of him that "he exulted in the free grace of God. His joy was contagious. Men leaped out of darkness into light, and lived a Christian life afterwards." Those words came from an English pastor, R.W. Dale, and the man he described was Dwight L. Moody.

This "open secret" seems to have a special effect on other people. As for us, it has no direct effect on our standing with God, or our sanctification or glorification, but it has a lot to do with how we enjoy these privileges.

That is what this book is all about.

T W O

Whose Idea Was This?

*Where love radiates its joy, there
we have a feast.*

—JOHN CHRYSOSTOM

∾

THE SECRET OF JESUS WAS—and is—His inner joy. That is
the message of this book. Many intimations in the New
Testament lead us to believe that while in our midst, Jesus had
a cheerful disposition and a merry heart.

Here is what Gilbert Chesterton wrote at the close of his book
Orthodoxy:[1] "He [Jesus] concealed something. . . . He restrained
something. . . . There was something that He hid from all men
. . . some one thing that was too great for God to show us when
He walked upon our earth; and I have sometimes fancied that it
was His mirth."

That is a fascinating suggestion, with all kinds of ingenious
ramifications. Even so, had I the temerity to respond, I would
dare to suggest that mirth is only part of the secret. Mirth
according to the dictionary is spontaneous amusement, manifested briefly. It is a pleasant temporary expression of a disposition to hilarity or glee. By contrast, the joy of the Lord is
actually a fruit of the Holy Spirit, and is therefore a radiant condition of the soul.

Jesus' soul condition is described by my actor friend, Bruce Marchiano, in these sparkling words which I have borrowed from his recent book *In the Footsteps of Jesus*:

> Yes, Jesus smiled; yes, Jesus laughed. Jesus smiled wider and laughed heartier than any human being who has ever walked the planet. He was young. He radiated good cheer. The real Jesus was a man of such merriment, such gladness of heart, such freedom and openness, that He proved irresistible. He became known through Galilee for His genuine strength, the sparkle in His eyes, the spring in His gait, the heartiness in His laugh, the genuineness of His touch; His passion, playfulness, excitement, and vitality: His JOY! He made a dazzling display of love. He set hearts afire. He was an elated, triumphant young man with an incredible quality of life . . . so different from the solemn religious types He constantly encountered.

We ourselves may also express the joy of the Lord in smiles and laughter and good cheer, but those are not the only ways. We participate in His joy through acts of worship, praise, prayer, and song, in witnessing to the saving grace of God and in helping others.

One statement in the Gospel of Luke will illustrate what I mean. It will bring us close to what I call Jesus' secret. "At that time Jesus, full of joy through the Holy Spirit, said, 'I praise you, Father'" (Luke 10:21 NIV). That verse brings together God the Father, the Son of God, the Holy Spirit, and joy in worship.

Such a verse (and others like it) clearly suggest that our Lord Jesus was equipped with a buoyant disposition. If so, where did He get it? From what Source? On the human side, of course, there was His mother Mary, a true daughter of the Hebrew race. The Hebrew people have always been known as a joyous, singing, festive people. To this the Old Testament bears faithful witness, for beyond its inspired history and prophecy it contains the record of a great people's songs and celebrations.

Christians who have tapped the secret of Jesus' inner joy like to think it came from an even more profound source—namely, from heaven. According to our scriptural authorities, heaven is the fountainhead for all such blessings: "Every good gift and every perfect gift is from above" (James 1:17). Where else could joy have originated?

The Gospel of Luke tells us that before Mary was wed to Joseph, the angel Gabriel paid her a visit.[2] He informed her that the Holy Spirit would come upon her, and that the power of the Most High would overshadow her. She would then bear a son whose name was Jesus, and He would be called the Son of the Highest. The Gospel of Matthew also says that an angel also told Joseph that Mary would give birth to a Son, whom Joseph would name Jesus, because He would save His people from their sins.[3]

When Mary went to visit her cousin Elizabeth prior to the birth of Jesus, Luke says that she declared, "My soul magnifies the Lord, and my spirit has *rejoiced* in God my Savior!"[4] Is anything more beautiful than Luke's story of the first Christmas, when the joy of the angels filled the air above Bethlehem? Today Christmas is the celebration of the birth of Jesus, at which time we recall the wondrous signs that accompanied that event, and especially the message of the angels bringing "good tidings of great joy . . . to all people."[5]

Later, in the unfolding of Scripture to the church, Jesus became recognized not only as the Son of God, but also as the Second Person of the Godhead and the Logos or Word who was in the beginning with God. Such profound theological concepts are not easily grasped by the human mind. To take them in, in order that we might look for the source of joy in Jesus' life, it becomes necessary to go back not merely to the first century, nor to the antediluvian or Mesozoic or Paleozoic eras, nor even to the beginning of time itself, but farther back—into eternity.

Let me invite you to step out on the patio of our modest home. It is a clear, beautiful night. Just for a moment let us forget the problems that face us and gaze up at the moon, the stars, and the planets. As we watch we see the majestic Power of the universe at work, and we find it easy to attribute personality to this mighty Power. We love Him. He is our God, whom we Christians call Father. He is the Creator and Sustainer of the universe.

Psalm 19 begins with these thrilling words:

> The heavens declare the glory of God,
> and the firmament shows His handiwork.

Not everyone has such a poetic view of the cosmic beginning. In fact many people, when they get a good look at the starry heavens on a clear night, say they feel uncomfortable. Creation to them is a baffling puzzle. If they wonder, "Whose idea was all this anyway?" they probably dismiss the thought with "What does it have to do with me?"

Well, whose idea *was* it? When we turn to Revelation 4 we find the answer. John the apostle tells us that when in the Spirit on the island of Patmos, he saw four living creatures giving glory and honor and thanks before the throne of the Lord God Almighty. He also saw 24 elders, each bowing down before the throne and worshiping God with the words (in the King James version) "O Lord . . . thou hast created all things, and for thy pleasure they are and were created."[6]

This word of praise seems to give us a hint as to why God brought about the creation: *He is God!* He does as He pleases. He is beholden to no one and is in no one's pocket. He created the universe in the first place not primarily to demonstrate His power or to declare His glory (which He does magnificently), but simply to fulfill His personal desire by doing something that gave Him pleasure. Surely one can infer from the elders' praise that they understood that deep within the heart of God is a joy expressing itself in His mighty acts of creation.

We humble mortals, when we are in a creative mood, easily recognize the presence of joy that comes along with our own creativity. Not for nothing did God make us in His image and likeness! Augustine writes in his *Confessions* that in his search for God he went to the "crawling things" of the sea and asked them to tell him something about God. In response they all cried out with a loud voice, "He made us!"[7] The book of Job tells us that when the creation took shape, the morning stars sang together and "all the sons of God shouted for joy" (Job 38:7).

I love the way my friend Dr. Shadrach Meshach Lockridge, one of America's great preachers, describes the forming of the universe. He says with a straight face, "God came from nowhere because there was nowhere for Him to come from. And coming from nowhere, He stood on nothing because there was nowhere for Him to stand. And standing on nothing, He reached out where there was nothing to reach, caught something when there was nothing to catch, and hung something on nothing and told it to stay there!"

So God, if our understanding of the text in Revelation is correct, hung something on nothing, and brought creation into existence and continues to sustain it. He did all this for His own pleasure, because He desired to do it. Not for power, not for glory, but for joy.

Didn't He?

THREE

Where Did He Get It?

Sun and moon bow down before Him,
All who dwell in time and space.
Alleluia! Alleluia!
Praise with us the God of Grace!

—HENRY LYTE[1]

∾

IN ONE OF HIS MOST significant utterances, Jesus gave this word of cheer to His disciples: "Do not fear, little flock, for it is your Father's good pleasure to give you the kingdom."[2] How much do we know about the Father's good pleasure "which He purposed in Himself"? We humans often take pleasure in putting things together; why should not God the Creator take joy in what the psalmist calls the "work of His fingers"? Listen to these words in Isaiah and Zephaniah:

> Be glad and rejoice forever in what I create. [3]

> He will quiet you with His love, He will rejoice over you with singing.[4]

When I meditate on the opening words of Genesis, I think I hear the music of the morning stars. Let us go one better than the airline that claims to fly in "friendly skies." Let us believe

27

that God put a song of gladness in outer space, that the mighty galaxies themselves are expressing cosmic joy:

> . . . forever singing, as they shine,
> "The hand that made us is divine!" [5]

Our first premise, based on faith, is that the cosmos we know, the universe of which we can see only a tiny portion through the Hubble telescope, is an expression of love and joy by the Creator. This premise is predicated on the Word of Truth in the Bible, which proclaims that God is love. We can say that God invented the smile if we like, and that He invented human laughter, but we cannot say He invented love because He *is* love. The mighty machinery of the galaxies is the expression of His love. The joy implanted by the Creator God Himself acting out of love became the joy that caused the morning stars to sing together.

Before we leave the mysteries of eternity, let us think again about the One who brought into being this magnificent expanse of creation. Theologians have deduced, not from spatial considerations but from their understanding of divine revelation in the Bible, a number of attributes of God which they consider self-evident. These attributes they call divine perfections. The list varies from one theologian to another and one creed to another, but it usually includes the following: God is infinite, eternal, immutable, illimitable, immortal, all-wise, all-knowing, all-goodness, spiritual, holy, sovereign, righteous, gracious, merciful, loving, and true.

Did you notice an omission from the list? What about joy? Is not joy an attribute of God? For some reason joy seems to have been overlooked or muted, if not actually ignored in theological studies and writings since the days of the apostles. A quick look on any seminary or Bible college library shelf is sufficient to convince the casual researcher of the absence of joy.

Yet surely joy is not incompatible with any of the attributes in the above compendium. If God is perfect holiness, is He not also perfect joy? If He is love, does He not express His love joyously?

My conclusion is that at least some respected members of the scholarly community do not consider joy to be an attribute of God. Perhaps they think that attributing joy to God is (as Freud would say) an anthropomorphism. I submit that this opinion seems unsupported by Scripture, which tells us in many ways and places that "God is love" and "the joy of the Lord is your strength."

Scientists sometimes refer to the material cosmos around us, with all its dimensions and facets, as the "given." If we should ask some members of the scientific community whether love and joy are present in the "given," they would turn toward us with a rather odd look. What? Love on Arcturus and Betelgeuse? Joy on the moons of Uranus?

The response would be in the negative; we would be informed that the universe is totally insensitive to such emotional qualities. The cosmos is there—it is a datum open to scrutiny as to what it is—but it tells us nothing about origins: where it came from or why it exists. As for such things as love and joy, we might look for them among a random assortment of human beings, but nowhere else.

But here is an interesting sidelight. Many of the scientists of the past and present who have been exploring the universe believe there is "more out there" than the material facts show. As they see it, the sum of the data, when taken together, is greater than the data in the computer. They are convinced that God does in fact reveal Himself in love, that the universe was created in goodness and is an expression of divine pleasure and joy.

For one reason or another, many of these scientists are unable to express their faith freely in the classroom, but it is nonetheless genuine. They would, I think, agree with the premise of this book: that the entire Godhead—Father, Son, and Holy Spirit—express the joy that is inherent in what God has created, and that when He condescended to dwell upon the earth, our Lord Jesus Christ drew upon that joy in becoming the

Redeemer of the human race. How that occurred is beyond our humble capacity to imagine. What we see in the Gospels is simply the evidence.

Having looked at the vastness of the outer reaches of our Father's creation, let us now open the record and see how Jesus went about His mission. We will start by examining His personality. Hang on! It should prove interesting.

The Man
of Joy

FOUR

The Merry Jesus

It is the heart that is unsure of its God
that is afraid to laugh.

—GEORGE MACDONALD

∽

IN THE YEAR 1514 SOMEONE published a sensational forgery in Venice, Italy, purporting to be a description of Jesus Christ by one Publius Lentulus. This Lentulus was said to have been the Roman procurator of Judea either before or after Pontius Pilate. The Lentulus family actually was prominent in the ancient Roman Empire, and one member is recorded as being governor of the province of Syria 60 years before Christ.

"Publius Lentulus," however, never existed except in the fertile mind of some medieval perpetrator of hoaxes.

Nevertheless the phony document has been widely circulated throughout Europe down even to our own time. It was titled "The Epistle of Lentulus to the Roman Senate," and the description of Jesus of Nazareth follows in English translation, as I found it in the rare book room of the Library of Congress:

> He is a tall man, well shaped and of an amiable and revered aspect; his hair is of a color that can hardly be matched, falling into graceful curls . . . parted on the

crown of his head, running as a stream to the front after the fashion of the Nazarenes; his forehead high, large and imposing; his cheeks without spot or wrinkle, beautiful with a lovely red; his nose and mouth formed with exquisite symmetry; his beard, of a color suitable to his hair, reaching below his chin and parted in the middle like a fork; his eyes bright blue, clear and serene. . . . [1]

In the next paragraph appears the statement "No man has seen him laugh," which has had an astonishing impact on the church.

Bruce Barton described the counterfeit document in his book *The Man Nobody Knows*, published in 1926.[2] Barton told of reading a contemporary English book in which the author said he visited a certain "Lord Fisher" (probably Sir Norman F.W. Fisher) and found him depressed in spirit. The usually lively English lord had just come across the bogus Lentulus statement and it had shaken his faith as a Christian. Said his visitor, "To worship a Lord who never laughed—it was a strain, and Lord Fisher made no pretence about that."

The inference here is that Jesus never did laugh, and therefore humor, which does so much to alleviate the stress of our daily existence, had no part in our Lord's life. Barton said that the Lentulus forgery "robbed the world of the joy and laughter of the friendliest man who ever lived." The document implied further that since we are followers of Jesus, presumably humor should have no place in our lives either.[3]

This fabricated document is not only laughable, but it is theologically unsound. Orthodox doctrine since the Council of Chalcedon (A.D. 451) has held that Jesus Christ is "perfect in Godhead and also perfect in manhood; truly God and truly man, of a reasonable soul and body . . . in all things like to us, without sin." "All things" includes laughter! How could Jesus be truly man without laughing at some of the incongruous things that happen in life, like this duplicitous letter? If Jesus wept, He also laughed. Laughter is one of the characteristics that distinguish humans from the primates. It is also a characteristic of the kingdom of God—at least that is the way I read the apostle Paul. He wrote to the Romans, "The kingdom of God is . . . joy in the Holy Spirit" (14:17).

If given half a chance in any era, genuine human joy naturally expresses itself in merriment. Not in ridicule, or mocking, or jeering, or off-color stories, but in the playful expressions of people making light of the bumpy circumstances of life and having fun with each other. Many of us have worked for a living in atmospheres where the banter was objectionable, but thank God there are also Christian groups and bands where merry spirits can take their difficulties in stride and even "count them all joy," and where the unexpected blessings of heaven bring shouts of "Hallelujah!"

An old Shaker philosopher, Brother Calvin Fairchild, put it this way: "Some people think it vulgar to laugh, but let such stand in life's gloomy shadows if they choose. As a general rule the best men and women laugh the most. Good, round, side-shaking laughter is healthy for everybody."

Plenty of merriment is recorded in the Old Testament as the Israelite people enjoyed their festivals. There was also merriment in New Testament times, if one cares to look for it. Jesus Himself, as a true Man of Joy, had a merry outlook on life. A few books have been written describing our Lord's wit, His repartee, His keen sense of the absurd (the camel and the needle's eye), and His ability to see the comical side of many a human situation or predicament. I have found that even when no humor whatever was involved, as in the accounts of Jesus' conversations with the woman at the well and the woman taken in adultery, the dialogues carry a unique style, a twist and a flair that betray the Master's touch. His good-natured approach to life seems to have been rooted in a great inner joy.

Thus when His contemporaries accused our Lord of being a "winebibber" (what we would call a "wino"), He laughed it off. When they reproached His disciples because they did not fast, He said they couldn't because they were part of a wedding party. When He was compared unfavorably to His friend John the Baptist, He grasped the opportunity to praise John. When His disciples were accused of violating the Sabbath by plucking ears of grain, Jesus took delight in pointing out that David once violated the same law at Nob by eating the sacred bread which Ahimelech told him was reserved for priests, and then passing it out to his troops.[4]

What do you suppose was the attraction that caused the Galilean fishermen to leave their nets and follow Jesus? What made Levi the tax collector abandon his booth and cash box to join His team? One answer might be: Jesus was a man of such joy, such merriment, such gladness of Spirit, such freedom and openness that He was irresistible. Today that may seem hard to visualize, but in ancient Palestine it is clear that people wanted to be near Him, to catch His bright spirit, and if possible to learn His secret, to share His joy and join in what He was doing for other people.

My pastor, Dr. Michael MacIntosh, has captured this spirit of joy accurately in his book *The Tender Touch of God*:

> The joy of the Lord was at the tomb of the resurrected Lazarus, overshadowing the sadness and disappointment of the dead man's sisters. Joy was there when the leper returned to thank Jesus. Joy was there when a woman caught in the very act of adultery was forgiven and released from her sin. Joy was there when the deaf heard, the blind saw, and the lame walked. Joy was there on the mountainside as the multitudes listened to the profound teachings of Jesus. Joy was there when the little children flocked to Jesus. Joy was there when the boy gave Jesus his lunch so that He could work a miracle and feed the thousands. Joy was there when Jesus forgave Zacchaeus for abusing his authority. Joy was there when Jesus stood up in the boat and stopped the storm. Joy was there when dawn broke and the women knew that Jesus was resurrected from the dead. Everywhere Jesus went, joy tagged along.[5]

Most pictorial representations of Jesus show Him looking serious, mournful, even weeping in agony of spirit and body, or else grim, resolute, and defiant. The very thought of His appearing in a lighthearted or jocular mood is evidently shocking to some religious minds. A merry Jesus seems to such to be offensive and sacrilegious. The creeds and catechisms of the church have taken great pains to enshrine the biblical truths for us, but in their sedate form they may have omitted important aspects of the man Christ Jesus.

The rank and file of Christians have done better down the years. They seem to have caught something of the Man of Joy and His message of good cheer. Even totally unchurched folk have been known to admire Jesus as a "good guy," an "upbeat Person who got set up." But normally the solemn religious element continues to dominate and the joy is lost.

Billy Graham wrote in *The Secret of Happiness*, "We never hear of Jesus laughing, though I am sure He did."[6] Above everything else, what convinces me that Jesus laughed is the fact that when people are "in Christ" they also begin to laugh.

Luke records one priceless scene when the Holy Spirit filled Jesus with merriment. He had sent out 70 evangelists to the cities and towns He intended to visit. They now returned from their tour exuberant over the results of their preaching. Were they laughing? Of course they were laughing. It was at this point, Luke writes, that Jesus captured the true hilarity of the scene when He said, "I praise You, Father, Lord of heaven and earth, that You have hidden these things from the wise and prudent and have revealed them to babes."[7]

The Bible reminds us again and again of the "voice of mirth." The book of Proverbs says that "the merry heart has a continual feast," and that such a heart is "good" medicine. The psalmist sings, "Then our mouth was filled with laughter." In another psalm he speaks of "God my exceeding joy." How do we express exceeding joy? What do we do? We laugh! Isaiah exults, "Sing, O heavens! Be joyful, O earth!" Jeremiah describes the "voice of joy and the voice of gladness . . . of the bridegroom and . . . bride." Jesus told His disciples that after He left them "your grief will turn to joy . . . [which] no one will take away." The apostle Peter declares that the Christians to whom he is writing "are filled with an inexpressible and glorious joy."

In the twelfth chapter of the letter to the Hebrews is a verse that gives an unusually clear insight into our Lord's mental attitude as He began His ministry. The verse reads, "Let us fix our eyes on Jesus . . . who for the joy set before him endured the cross, scorning its shame, and sat down at the right hand of the throne of God" (12:2 NIV). Joy? What joy? The joy of heaven, of course.

"Don't worry about tomorrow," Jesus advised His disciples. "Your heavenly Father knows what your needs are." To Peter's question about John's future prospects Jesus replied, "What's it to you? You follow me." And to the brothers who were quarreling over their inheritance He said simply, "Who made me a judge over you?" In each incident there was perhaps a twinkle in His eye.

Because of heaven, Jesus could take what He had to face on earth. Because of the thrill and wonder of eternity, He could run the crossfire of time. Because of the glory of God His Father, He could put up with the sinful pride and unbelievable mistakes of the children of men. And because of the presence of the Holy Spirit in Him, He could carry the buoyancy of His eternal joy with Him into the time zone of Palestine, sharing it with others while carrying out His Father's will. "Be of good cheer"—that is, "Courage! Brighten up!" He told His disciples, "There are tribulations in this life, but I have overcome the world."[8]

As Professor John Knox says, Jesus was "a Man of incomparable moral insight, understanding and imagination, of singular moral purpose and integrity, of extraordinary moral courage and ardor, of intense devotion to duty, and of joyous trust in God. Although He took His life very seriously, there is no reason to think He took it solemnly; perhaps He took it too seriously to take it solemnly. . . . He faced the whole gamut of human life with absolute fidelity and with freshness and great good humor. . . . He believed that what is beautiful and good in this world and in human life is to be enjoyed without apology."[9]

Consider the way Jesus conducted Himself with children. He actually rebuked His disciples for being killjoys and interfering when the children climbed on His back (as they probably did) and tugged at His beard and kissed Him. What a merry time!

Women, sick people, and people of other races and cultures all came to Him with their troubles because they knew they would be treated with gentleness, respect, compassion, and love.

In a hundred places the Bible tells us that the message of salvation in Christ is a message of love bathed in joy. The very word *gospel* means "good news, glad tidings." The Westminster Shorter Catechism declares that the chief end of man (or as we would say, humanity) is to glorify God and enjoy Him forever. I'll let my friends who are better qualified tell you how to glorify Him. My aim is to get you to enjoy Him.

FIVE

Uncommon Wedding

Keep company with the more cheerful sort of the godly; there is no mirth like the mirth of believers.

—RICHARD BAXTER

∾

YOU AND I ARE INVITED to a delightful place where there is joy and laughter. The place is Cana, a village of Galilee, where a wedding ceremony is about to begin.[1] Jesus and His mother are among the invited guests, and so are the disciples, which of course includes us. That is, some of us. Others of us have been there for some time, preparing for the festivities.

It is a lovely occasion and everyone is smiling. Excitement fills the air. The ceremony is being held outdoors in the sunshine. The presence of Jesus lends a sudden touch of glory to the proceedings. Can you imagine anything more thrilling than just being there?

Why do you suppose Jesus was invited to this event? Was it because He wore a sad expression? No. What a misreading of His real character! If I read Scripture correctly, Jesus was an attractive person with a contagious personality—just the kind of individual that people like to be around. He exhibited a light and serene spirit. He radiated cheer. According to the letter to the Hebrews, He was anointed by His Father with the oil of gladness more than His companions.[2]

That's why Jesus was invited to the wedding. Not because He was a relative they had to invite. Not because He was an apostle of doom and gloom. Not because He was sure to go about gratuitously buttonholing the other guests and informing them that the fires of hell awaited them. He was invited because He was someone special—a Gentleman, a lovable Person, and a very warm Friend.

How does this picture compare with other Scriptures that tell us Jesus was "a man of sorrows and acquainted with grief"?[3] Let's note right away that the sorrows and griefs that came later in His ministry in fulfillment of prophecy were not of His own devising. He knew about them, but at the wedding they seem to have played no part in His temperament. When they came, they were thrust upon Him from without. He would be ready for them; but this wedding took place early in His ministry, and at the moment He was not borrowing trouble or taking thought for the morrow.

Here then is the real Jesus—young, fresh, and enthusiastic, setting out on His heavenly assignment to our planet to bring relief to the hard-pressed human race. What a mission! I recall from my younger days a popular ballad about Casey Jones, a legendary locomotive engineer who, after being assigned to a dangerous run between Lynchburg and Danville, Virginia, "mounted to the cabin with his orders in his hand." At His baptism Jesus had His orders in His hand. He knew that He was facing a very rough ride, but He was not dismayed or depressed. The New Testament tells us it was because of "the joy that was set before Him [that He] endured the cross, despising the shame."[4]

Our Lord came from heaven to bring salvation to the world, and after His excruciating ordeal of sacrifice He went back to heaven to reign forever, but with the promise that He would be coming again to earth. His Father sent Him to us to preach the kingdom of God, to set us free from our sins, and to prepare us for a place in glory. He faced spiritual wickedness in high places, and He proved ready and eager to do battle with them.

At the wedding Jesus is stopped by His mother as He walks by her. She tells Him, "They have run out of wine."[5] Many people have difficulty in understanding Jesus' reply. I see Him putting His hands on His mother's shoulders and saying with a loving twinkle in His eye, "Woman, what am I going to do with you? It's not my time!" (When Dostoevsky described this scene in *The Brothers Karamazov*, he added, "He [Jesus] must have smiled gently at her.)

In a culture where women were classified as chattel, Jesus always treated women with gentleness, respect, and dignity. The same could be said of His treatment of people of other races— the Roman centurion, the Canaanite woman. As for the sick and infirm, He didn't wring His hands over them; He just healed them.

Mary may be experiencing a premonition of what is coming, for she says to the servants (remember, you and I are there and we have chosen to help the servants), "Do whatever he tells you."[6] And shortly Jesus orders the big stone waterpots to be filled with water. We do it. Then He tells us to draw off some of the water and take it to the host. We do that.

The host tastes what we bring him and his eyebrows go up.

He calls over the bridegroom and asks him, "What's going on?" Well, it happens that you and I saw what was going on. We poured the water into those jars. We were aware that the Lord Jesus was doing something *as God* with the processes of nature. We knew, we knew! But the very nature of the miracle was such that in spite of its awesomeness we were ecstatic.

C.S. Lewis suggests that to understand this and other miracles, we need first to believe in some reality beyond nature, beyond the universe itself.[7] He says, "There is an activity of God displayed throughout creation. The universe itself is one great miracle." He then takes us back to earth: "The miracles done by God incarnate, living as a man in Palestine (that is, Jesus), perform the same things as this wholesale activity [in creation], but at a different speed and on a smaller scale." In other words, "the miracles . . . do small and quick" what God is always doing in His creation. The same miraculous activity that operates the universe, for example, was employed by Jesus at the feeding of the five thousand to make little bread into much bread.[8]

Year after year the Sovereign God creates wine through the grapevine, grain through the wheatstalk, babies through natural begetting. Lewis claims that when miracles occur, the New Testament record shows consistently that God was using ordinary nature as a channel for "supernature." He used water miraculously to create wine, and bread and fish to multiply bread and fish. As for healing, when God enters the natural order to perform a healing miracle, His divine energy uses the natural organs of the body. "Stretch out your hand," Jesus said one Sabbath day to a man with a withered hand. He did, and the hand was miraculously restored.[9]

To understand fully what took place at Cana, I believe, we have to be in on Jesus' secret. He was a Man of Joy, remember? He carried an easy burden and operated with a light heart. It's hard for us to bear that fact in mind because we are so used to the man-made "holy" depictions of Him amid heavy religious solemnities.

Perhaps, since He found Himself at a wedding party, Jesus decided on a little merrymaking of His own. Customarily at Mideastern social festivities the best wine was served to the guests first; later on something akin to "rotgut" was reserved for those well along who kept coming back for more. Jesus turned things around, as He often did. He brought in the best at the last—a prophetic touch, highly amusing and rather startling, but the wedding seems to have gained greatly by it. Quite possibly He did it to honor His friends, the bride and groom.

The text says that Jesus conveyed a sign to the marriage celebrants. What did it signify? Perhaps He was symbolizing the message of the Gospel, telling them that He came to earth to change the water of ordinary conventional religion into the wine of joy and love in the Spirit by His direct action as God.

Perhaps He thought beyond that, to Pentecost, to the time when the Spirit of God would be "given," and He would touch our spirits with His own holy flame, turning our individual lives into vessels of joy and laughter and good news and *agape* love for everybody. I'm sure He looked to that ultimate Great Day after all the tribulation when the kingdom would come, and we would relax from our struggling and worrying and complaining, and break out the tambourines. Abundant living! Joy!

Meanwhile as we enter the new millennium the Holy Spirit is still pouring out love into individual lives. The ugly spirits of resentment, hostility, and bitterness are being dissolved by a divine solvent tipped from heaven into the heart. Reading the Bible for some people is no longer a tedious chore but is becoming a feasting on the Word. Worship is becoming a joyous celebration. The casual churchgoer is becoming a believer, an object of grace and a tributary of love. The water has become wine—not the alcoholic drug, but the wine of a contented heart, the wine of peace and gladness.

In a hundred places the Bible tells us that the message of salvation in Christ is not of judgment but a message of love and joy. The very words "evangel" and "gospel" mean "good news, glad tidings." Many of the great hymns of the faith that we sing so majestically are really effusions of joy.

What is joy? It is the enjoyment of God and the good things that come from the hand of God. If our new freedom in Christ is a piece of angel food cake, joy is the frosting. If the Bible gives us the wonderful words of life, joy supplies the music. If the way to heaven turns out to be an arduous steep climb, joy rigs up the chairlift.

The fact is that joy is an attribute of God Himself. It brings with it pleasure, gladness, and delight. Joy is merriment without frivolity, hilarity without raucousness, and mirth without cruelty. Joy is sportive without being rakish and festive without being cheap. Joy radiates animation, sparkle, and buoyancy. It is more than fun, yet it has fun. It expresses itself in laughter and elation, yet it draws from a deep spring that keeps flowing long after the laughter has died and the tears have come. Even while it joins those who mourn, it remains cheerful in a world that has gone gray with grief and worry.

Joy is not a sentimental word. It has a clean tang and bite to it, the exhilaration of mountain air. It blows away the dustiness of our days with a fresh breeze, and makes life more carefree. Perhaps the French translators of the Bible were attempting to say something like that when they rendered the third beatitude "Blessed are the debonair, for they shall inherit the earth."[10] The French apparently see a carefree quality in meekness and humility that most of us miss. And is joy carefree? Is joy "debonair"—that is, lighthearted, genial, and gracious? You decide.

Goethe at the age of 75 admitted that he had known only four weeks of happiness. There are Christians, some of them victims of lifelong suffering, who could say almost the same thing about happiness. But joy! Here we move into a different dimension, and that telltale light comes into the eye of the believer. Joy is the joy of salvation, the exultation of God's Spirit in men and women, "good measure, pressed down, shaken together, and running over."[11]

Joy was part of Jesus' ministry while He was on earth; it was a joy both present and in prospect. For today's Christian, fulfillment is never quite complete in this "vale of tears," but there is always joy in prospect. Thus joy becomes the ecstasy of eternity in a soul that has made its peace with God and is ready to do His will, here and hereafter.

At Cana the wedding vows have been exchanged and the wedding rites are over. A jubilant crowd escorts the bride and groom to their new home. The text says, "This beginning of signs Jesus did in Cana of Galilee, and manifested His glory; and His disciples believed in Him."[12] Thus heaven smiled on Jesus' first miracle.

What is to keep us from this kind of enjoyment? I don't know. I am no prophet. I have no pill to offer on the market that will produce a sunny disposition and a light heart. But I can pray that you will be saved by the blood of Jesus and filled with the Holy Spirit so that He will give you joy. I know that route.

SIX

Religious Smog

Words of joy are like sluice gates; open them and floods pour through.

—AMY CARMICHAEL

❧

YEARS AGO WHILE I WAS serving a student pastorate in northern California, a teenage girl in our church group, whose name I have forgotten, asked me a question. She said she was going with a boy of a different faith (a fact I already knew) and that certain aspects of church teaching were creating a problem in their relationship. She said she had been to see his pastor, who, after he heard her out, said to her, "My dear, don't you know we're put into this world to suffer?"

I have since then found a remarkably similar statement in Thackeray's nineteenth-century English novel *The Newcomes*. A French priest tries to comfort a long-suffering wife with the words "Not here, my daughter, is to be your happiness. Whom heaven loves it afflicts."

My teenage friend's question to me was "Do you think that's right?"

Let me use that girl's question as a springboard to plunge into the real issue, which involves the whole mystery of existence on earth. Her friend's pastor was correct this far: We are

47

born into a world full of suffering, much of which seems to come upon us with no explanation. But does the Bible, the Word of God, really teach that our *purpose* in being born is to suffer? Or is that just some religious smog?

To put it into more precise doctrinal terms, does Christianity teach that when God created the human race, He predestined it (or most of it, babies included) to eternal misery by His inscrutable will? Or does it teach that God became so angry over the sin of Adam and Eve that He condemned the whole human race to work out its punishment here on this planet through suffering? Think a minute. Is that really the Good News of the Gospel? Is that the "kingdom" Jesus was talking about? And when He said, "I have come that they may have life, and have it more abundantly," is that what He meant?

Earlier I suggested that Jesus' inner joy came directly from the heart of His heavenly Father by the Holy Spirit, and that on the human side His genial nature probably was inherited from His mother, who was the daughter of a race known and honored the world over for its cheerfulness, vivacity, and ability to laugh even in the most deeply trying circumstances. (Think of the contributions of Jewish comedians.)

Now I would like to suggest a third source of Jesus' joy: God's written Word, the Old Testament.

Let us begin with the Psalms, which Jesus seems to have loved and which He often quoted. When I sat down one day and began seriously to look for love and joy in that book, I became so excited I was (to borrow a phrase my mother often used) "beside myself." In particular I found various forms of the words joy, joyous, enjoy, delight, gladness, exuberance, and jubilation appearing well over a hundred times, beginning with Psalm 1 and ending with a musical turn-on in Psalm 150. I am informed that one scholar has listed 13 Hebrew roots and 27 separate words for joy in the Old Testament.

After reading the Psalms in my personal devotions for half a century, I was under the common impression that most of them were rather plaintive in character, reflecting the hardships and struggles of Palestinian existence. I now realize that nothing could be further from the truth!

The Psalms are above all else hymns of praise and thanksgiving that give a sweet savor and rich perfume to life. They radiate cheer and exhilaration; they sparkle with zest and high spirits. If we have missed that (and for a long time I did), it may be because for centuries we have associated them with a liturgical form that majors on veneration and awe rather than joy.

But the Psalms are not dirges or wails; overwhelmingly they are the exuberant outpouring of writers who are literally kicking up their heels, so excited are they to discover the redemptive love of Almighty God. "Shout for joy!" "Praise Him with the clash of cymbals." "Praise Him with tambourine and dancing." "Make music to Him." "Praise Him, sun and moon." "Extol the Lord." "My heart leaps for joy." "In Your name I will lift up my hands." "The hills are clothed with gladness." "The valleys . . . shout for joy and sing."

Let's continue our quest by researching some other Old Testament Scriptures.

We hear God speaking to the prophet Isaiah in these words: "Shout for joy, O heavens; rejoice, O earth; burst into song, O mountains!" and again, "I will make you . . . the joy of all generations." Nehemiah writes, "The joy of the Lord is your strength." Zephaniah declares, "The Lord . . . will rejoice over you with singing." Even the sardonic preacher in Ecclesiastes says plainly, "God gives . . . joy."

For me it is difficult to call Jeremiah the "weeping prophet" after reading his glorious description of the blessing of God to come to the Jewish people when they returned from captivity in Babylon:

> For the LORD will ransom Jacob
>   and redeem them from the hand of those stronger
>   than they.
> They will come and shout for joy on the heights of
>   Zion; they will rejoice in the bounty of the Lord—
>   the grain, the new wine and the oil,
>   the young of the flocks and herds.

They will be like a well-watered garden,
   and they will sorrow no more.
Then maidens will dance and be glad,
   young men and old as well.
I will turn their mourning into gladness;
I will give them comfort and joy instead of sorrow.

—Jeremiah 31:11,12 NIV

Neither of the Old Testament nor the New can it be said that they reveal a God whose main purpose toward human beings was to afflict them with suffering. Just the opposite! He wished them the blessings of peace and love and joy in a land of fruitfulness and abundance.

In a gentle and affectionate way let us now look at the church that Jesus founded, and that we love today, albeit each in our own way. As the church moves into its third millennium, is it reflecting the tone of the book of Acts? Is it conveying the warm spirit of the early Christians, whose tremendous popularity spread all around the Mediterranean shores?

Or is it possible that the church has (unconsciously, perhaps) distilled much of the joy out of Christianity? Think of cherubic personalities like Francis of Assisi, or Brother Lawrence of the Resurrection, or Billy Bray, the Welsh lay preacher. How rare such apostles of joy have been in the annals of church history! Each was tremendously popular in his time, but the church seems hardly to have known what to do with them.

The Bible tells us that even the rivers and trees of the forest clap their hands in praise to God, but in many a church today hand-clapping is seldom practiced. It almost seems we have turned Isaiah inside out and exchanged the garment of praise for the spirit of heaviness. Joyfulness, lightheartedness, and jubilation seem out of order in many church assemblies. Joy gets scant treatment in our biblical and theological institutions and library indexes. Seldom does it creep into our creeds and church histories. It is nowhere to be seen in the records of religious wars, ecclesiastical disputes, inquisitions, and persecutions.

Today in many worship services the Psalms that are so full of gladness and blessedness are read aloud, but in a most ceremonious manner. It is not that joy is entirely ignored in the churches, for eloquent sermons are preached on the subject, and hymns are sung about it, but often the mood is reverently subdued. People do not expect to be lifted up. Many times their presence is due to childhood memories, or to a sense of duty and obligation. Even the young people who are loyal to their church in many cases expect nothing but solemnity when they enter its door.

Billy Graham states:

> One of the desperate needs among Christian young people is exuberance and vitality in their loyalty to Christ. People go to a football game today and shout their heads off, or go to a circus and cheer act after act. They become enthusiastic about everything conceivable, but when it comes to spiritual matters they think we are supposed to become sober and quiet, and wear black, and never have a good time or enjoy a religious event.[1]

Certainly a frivolous or jocular attitude is inappropriate in approaching the sacred mysteries of our faith, let alone the throne of God Himself. A sense of awe before the Shekinah Glory is an expression indispensable for true worship. But the problem with much worship today is not the departure of the divine Presence, for where two or three are gathered together in His name, Jesus still promises to be with us. Too often the problem is the supersanctimonious smog we spread over our church life, the unnecessary gravity with which our leadership protects its dignity, the unnatural posturing that can so easily pass into overbearing arrogance and conceit.

When I visited C.S. Lewis in Cambridge in 1963 he told me, "There is a great deal of false reverence about. There is too much solemnity and intensity in dealing with sacred matters, too much speaking in holy tones."[2] The tragic loss in all this pious gamesmanship is to the individual in the pew, who begins to feel that in the midst of the religious ceremonies he cannot get through to the Lord Himself. Recently I received a letter from a young lady in West Virginia saying, "It seems to me the subject of joy is sadly lacking in the lives of many Christians when we ought to be the most joyful people on the face of the earth."

When Christians try to act more holy than Jesus Himself, the church is in trouble. Jesus was particularly sharp with "scribes and Pharisees" who "for a pretense make long prayers."[3] Exit pomposity!

Add to the mix the seemingly endless protocol, minutiae, and irrelevata that tie our ecclesiastical proceedings in knots, and you have the church of the third millennium. To attend many church meetings today is to run the risk of humongous boredom.

Let me go further. Many of the authors of our Christian books seem unable to comprehend what it means to have the kind of radiant, overflowing, inner joy that Jesus brought to earth and shared with His followers. I have known professional theologians who appear baffled and bewildered by a demonstration of the believer's lighthearted joy in the Holy Spirit. To be set free by Jesus Christ, to revel in the new birth, to exude the joy of the Lord, to celebrate the knowledge that one's sins have been forgiven because of the vicarious sacrifice of Christ who went to the cross and shed His blood for us and our salvation, is to be—in their words—"an enthusiast." To explain such behavior, they compile erudite monographs about "cultic joy," "festal joy," and "eschatological joy."

But the joy that today's jubilant new convert has is no different from the joy that Jesus obviously had while He was ministering in Galilee and elsewhere, and which He shared with His disciples. This kind of reveling cannot be compartmentalized. It suffuses the whole of existence and blows the dismal clouds of unbelief out to sea. By a miracle of grace the Holy Spirit continues to make it available to us today. It is not mere jolliness, although fun and laughter cannot be ruled out of the kingdom. What Jesus actually brought with Him from heaven was something more than a new start for humanity; it was a clear, bubbling, unpolluted delight in God and God's creation, His redemption, His new creation, and His promise of eternal life.

I'm talking about the kind of divine joy that existed in paradise before the invasion of evil; or perhaps one was not aware that Adam and Eve were happy? Read the text again. Laughter was born in the Garden of Eden. Elisabeth Elliot reminds us that "obedience always leads finally to joy." Dr. Ed Wheat, a Christian marriage counselor, writes:

> As I put the principles of the Bible into practice, and as I learned how really to love my wife, this became pleasure as well as responsibility. Obedience took on the bright colors of joy.[4]

That aptly describes the true situation that existed in Eden at the beginning.

We shall be examining the biblical accounts, looking particularly at the people who were affected by the ministry of Jesus and those close to Him. The reason for this research is not simply to add to the massive scholarship that has already been posted in the New Testament field. The true reason for our study is to see whether this joy of the Lord can be appropriated today, not just by new converts in the first flush of rapture, but by all of us who love the Lord. Do we have access to it? Is there after all something in Christianity that can make our lives glow, that can turn sorrow into joy, discord into beautiful music, and dreariness into something fruitful? Did Jesus really bring something beautiful from heaven, something primordial out of the dawn of creation, that can give us the full radiance of life which we seem to keep missing?

In his remarkable book *The Way to Pentecost*, the well-known British Methodist preacher Samuel Chadwick tells us that he was "about my Heavenly Father's business" when—

in my search I came across a prophet, heard a testimony, and set out to seek I knew not what. I knew it was a bigger thing than I had ever known. It came along the line of duty, in a crisis of obedience. When it came I could not explain what had happened, but I was aware of things unspeakable and full of glory.

Some results were immediate. There came into my soul a deep peace, a thrilling joy, and a new sense of power. My mind was quickened. Every power was vitalized. There was a new sense of vitality, a new power of endurance. Things began to happen. It was as when the Lord Jesus stepped into the boat that with all the disciples' rowing had made no progress, and "immediately the ship was at the land." It was gloriously wonderful.

And then he points out that two thousand years ago something very similar happened to those who were present at Pentecost: "Illumination of mind, assurance of heart, intensity of love, fullness of power, exuberance of joy."

It was a vivid and authentic testimony by an outstanding servant of the Lord. Chadwick then declares that the Holy Spirit is—

the Spirit of Truth, the Spirit of Witness, the Spirit of Conviction, the Spirit of Power, the Spirit of Holiness, the Spirit of Life, the Spirit of Adoption, the Spirit of Help, the Spirit of Liberty, the Spirit of Wisdom, the Spirit of Revelation, the Spirit of Promise, the Spirit of Love, the Spirit of Meekness, the Spirit of Sound Mind, the Spirit of Grace, the Spirit of Glory, and the Spirit of Prophecy.[5]

Great! But not the Spirit of Joy? Why not? Luke tells us that Jesus came into Galilee after His baptism filled with the Spirit and preaching the kingdom of God. It was a message of good news and joy. The book of Acts adds that, during the days after Pentecost, the "disciples were filled with joy and with the Holy

Spirit."[6] They were having such a good time that people thought they were inebriated.

Now let's build a contrast. Perhaps you know of a church that is facing a serious crisis. At this moment, while you are reading this page, the church officers are meeting in grave session, trying to cope with a spiritual, moral, or financial issue that is threatening to divide the congregation. Other informal groups are meeting privately in homes to express their disaffection. Lengthy telephone calls are being made. Slander is being spread. Petitions are being prepared. Lawsuits are being threatened. Members reportedly have been seen attending other churches. As the officers of the congregation meet to grapple with the situation, no one would ever accuse them (as they did the early disciples) of being drunk. They are simply earnest Christians trying to make their way through their own religious smog.

How do we lovers of Jesus get into such entanglements? What must we do to be "regrafted," as Dr. Lloyd Ogilvie says, so that we can "catch the impact of the exhilarating elixir of Jesus' joy" as an "artesian flow," and "feel the palpable delight of His life?"

S E V E N

"Pecooler Noshuns"

Your religion is small pertaters, I must say.
You air in a dreary fog all the time.

—Artemus Ward

⌒

JESUS HAD A SENSE OF HUMOR. It's high time to excavate this truth and examine it objectively. It has been buried too long in the sludge of religious sobriety which is so often mistaken for reverence.

The Gospels abound with evidence pointing to the existence of Jesus' humor. His memorable sallies were forever bobbing to the surface in the sacred writings. No wonder His followers found it easy to copy them down! He described the teachers of the Jewish law as straining out a gnat and swallowing a camel. He said it was "easier for a camel to go through the eye of a needle than for a rich man to enter the kingdom of God." He described the care with which the religious leaders washed the outside of their cups before drinking from them, but left the inside soiled.

He pointed out how ludicrous it was to claim that He was casting out demons by the power of the head demon himself. He talked about blind men attempting to lead blind men, about dead people burying dead people, about picking figs off a thistle, about hiding a lamp under a bed. He figuratively laughed at people who were quick to point out the speck of dirt in someone else's eye while they had a two-by-four plank in their own.[1]

How much good humor was present, do you suppose, as Jesus called the youngsters to Himself and picked up the smallest ones and held them in His lap? Was there intimate talk? Banter? Laughter? Blessing? Did some mother who was present come up with raisin cakes for a treat? What do you think was actually going on when His disciples tried to break up the party?

Or consider the Canaanite woman who knelt at Jesus' feet and implored Him to heal her daughter of a demon possession.[2] This woman is elsewhere identified as a Syrophoenician, but today she would be called an Arab. Jesus looked down at the kneeling woman, and again His response was unexpected. He explained that His primary mission from God was to His own people Israel. Using a familiar analogy, He said, "The children's bread shouldn't be given to puppies." William Barclay suggests that here Jesus was "speaking with a smile."[3]

The woman looked up at Him and replied in the same light manner. "Yes, Lord, but even the puppies under the table eat the children's crumbs."

Although the text does not say so, what else could Jesus do but laugh? "You win," His attitude implied, and then He spoke those wonderful words: "The demon has left your daughter."

If Jesus had a sense of humor, what does that tell us about His Father? Christian faith looks upon Jesus, the risen Christ, as the Second Person of the Holy Trinity, and co-Creator with the Father. The late William R. Inge was known to Londoners as the "gloomy Dean of St. Paul's," but he was in great form when he wrote, "I have never understood why it would be considered derogatory to the Creator to suppose He has a sense of humor."[4]

More recently the beloved Quaker philosopher, D. Elton Trueblood, left us for the laughter of heaven. He wrote, "If Christ laughed a great deal, as the evidence shows, and if He is what He claimed to be, we cannot avoid the logical conclusion that there is laughter and gaiety in the heart of God."[5]

Books have been written about our Lord's wit, His repartee, His keen sense of the absurd, and His ability to see the comical side of a human situation or predicament. Even when no humor whatever is involved, His dialogue has a unique style, a twist and a flair that betray the Master's touch.

It is obvious that whatever sense of humor may be ascribed to Jesus was *good* humor. It derived not from cynicism or the bitterness of life, but rather from His naturally friendly approach to life. The Germans have a word "gemütlichkeit" or "good nature" which seems to fit Jesus' temperament. He comes through in the Gospel accounts as an attractive, loving personality, so different from the legalistic types He encountered during His ministry.

Look, for example, at the way He summoned His disciples. He visited some fishermen along the shore of the Sea of Galilee and said to them, "Follow me."[6] It is clear that this was not their first encounter with Jesus. The fact remains that they wasted no time in dropping their nets and taking off after Him. I can almost hear them saying to one another, "Why not?"

What attraction drew them? Was it His commanding appearance, the impressiveness of His voice of authority, the tempting prospects He set out for them, the poor conditions in the fishing industry, or some other persuasive factor? What made Levi the tax collector leave his booth and cash box and follow Jesus? Did he think Jesus was a rich man? A seer with second sight? An angel from God?

There is only one answer. Jesus was a man of such gladness of Spirit, such freedom and openness and magnetism in His attitude, that He was irresistible. They wanted to be near Him, to catch His Spirit, to do what He was doing for other people, and if possible to learn His secret.

What a pity that Jesus was not presented to succeeding generations as He presented Himself to His own: not as a holy, mystical figure but as a vital human person! We are told that great crowds of "common people" heard Him "gladly,"[7] and many accepted the Good News of the kingdom that He preached without realizing who He really was.

Today most pictorial representations of Jesus show Him grim and resolute, or else sad, suffering, in mortal agony, hanging from a cross. Anything else stirs distaste or resentment at the breaking of tradition. But to me here is what is sad: *The real Person of our Lord seldom comes through in the representations of Him through the ages.* The doctrine is there, to be sure. The creeds and catechisms have taken great pains to enshrine the biblical truths, but some of us think they have not done so well with the Stranger of Galilee.

It might be said that the rank and file of Christians have done better in capturing the personal essence of Jesus than have the august fathers of the church. Ordinary people sense something leveling, something winsome about the Man and His cheerful demeanor, while the traditionalists insist on emphasizing the elements of sanctimony and downplaying the joy.

I cannot help believing that Artemus Ward, Abraham Lincoln's favorite humorist, was reflecting the mind of Christ when he told the legalists of his day, "Your religion is small pertaters, I must say. You air in a dreary fog all the time, and you treat the jolly sunshine of life as though it were a thief, drivin' it from your doors by them pecooler noshuns of yourn." To which might be added a humorous word from Billy Sunday: "To see some people you would think that the essential of orthodox Christianity is to have a face so long you could eat oatmeal out of the end of a gas pipe."[8]

It is a wonder that so often in the history of the church the real Jesus does not come through. The New Testament itself is a document of great beauty, alive with joy, bright with cheerfulness, filled with love and excitement and healthy teaching for body and soul; yet for millions of people in generation after generation it remains a black-covered Book that tells people how bad they are. I know. I left it unopened for years just for that reason.

But what about those who open their Bibles and still fail to find the joy of the Lord? The reason, I believe, is that they are not filled with the Holy Spirit of God. And the reason they are not filled with God's Spirit is that they are loaded up with other, unholy spirits—that is to say, negative attitudes—and these spirits monopolize all the believer's time and energy. And what are they? Hostility, resentment, fear, antagonism, bitterness, envy, revenge, arrogance, self-love—the list goes on and on. How can one enjoy the fullness of the Spirit, who is God, when one is filled with everything else?

To be filled with the Spirit is to be filled with love. Love is the first fruit of the Spirit, and the second fruit is joy. To feel His love and know His joy, we need to become poor in spirit—in other words, to walk out of the junkyard and shut the gate.

But that spiritual state may not be what you think it is. To be poor in spirit means that we have shucked off the zeal so often compounded with corruptible human pride. We may not see it in ourselves, but other people do. They see us strutting like peacocks, seeking to draw attention. Get rid of it, Jesus is saying. Grow up. Become a full-grown person, mature, and operational.

As Irenaeus declared in the second century, "The glory of God is a man fully alive." He could have said the same thing about a woman—and added an exclamation point! But to be alive is to be alive in God, to be God-controlled, not to be a pious nothing with a handcrafted halo and a reputation for being "religious."

"Spiritual growth" is a term I personally fear, because I have learned that a lot of such growth consists simply in getting out of God's way. I'm certain God does not want me to develop into a spiritual giant even if I could. He wants me to become a spiritual pygmy so He can handle me. He wants me poor in spirit so He can do something with me without having to contend with my ever-present, darling ego.

It's when we let go of the rope that we discover that underneath are the everlasting arms. It is when we have no spirit at all, as far as the "flesh" is concerned, that we are able to receive the filling of the Holy Spirit. That is the work of the cross in Christian experience. As Paul wrote, "We have this treasure in earthen vessels, that the excellence of the power may be of God and not of us."[9]

Oh, the joy that comes when people realize that they don't have to be religious with God, they don't have to be sanctimonious, they don't have to be anything or do anything except repent and believe the Good News! All the blessing of the Father, the love of Jesus, and the joy of the Holy Spirit are theirs for the taking. Of such indeed is the kingdom of heaven.

The Hidden Secret

EIGHT

Surfing the Scriptures

Tell me what you find in the Bible,
and I will tell you what you are.

—Dr. Oskar Pfister

∽

WHAT IS THE PURPOSE OF the Bible? Or did it have a purpose? Why was it written? Scholars assure us it is nothing like the Koran, the work of one individual. Actually the Bible is a collection of inspired writings accumulated over a period of 1500 years.

But isn't there some purpose behind it? Yes, there is. Christians believe the Bible was written under divine inspiration to remove the barrier of sin from the human race and to reconcile us to our God, so that we might enjoy Him forever. The apostle Paul explains: "God was in Christ reconciling the world to Himself, not imputing their trespasses to them, and has committed to us the word of reconciliation."[1]

The Bible is the Holy Spirit's written "word of reconciliation." More than that, the Scriptures are God's love letter to the people of earth. For two thousand years men, women, and children have found it to be the key to life. Chapters and verses, nouns and verbs are so put together in God's Word that they convey cleansing, healing, forgiveness, and salvation to the human race. Thus for millions of believers the Bible continues to be a love gift to the human race, wrapped in the grace and tender mercy of God.

The New Testament tells us that "the law was given through Moses, but grace and truth came through Jesus Christ."[2] *Grace* means that our salvation was brought about by the sacrificial shedding of the blood of our Lord on the cross at Calvary. *Truth* is culminated by His death on our behalf and in our stead, followed by His resurrection from the grave. It might be said that here are the two most important facts of life ever revealed to humankind: namely, that Jesus died to take away sin, and that there is a life beyond.

As we read the Bible we discover a lot about ourselves. We were placed on this specially prepared planet by God's personal act of love, to enjoy its beauty and fruitful goodness, to care for it and for each other, and to live our lives in freedom and abundance. Charles Spurgeon wrote, "This fair world of ours was once a glorious temple, every pillar of which reflected the goodness of God, and every part of which was a symbol of good."[3]

So there was joy at creation; but then the Bible tells us frankly and candidly what happened to us. Through human temptations and the deceptions of the principalities and powers of darkness, the rapture of paradise was lost to humanity. Through human disobedience we spurned the divine blessing, turning it into a curse. Such is the teaching of the Bible.

There is no evading the facts; they declare themselves afresh each day in the headlines of the morning newspaper. Sin continues to harass individuals, bring families into turmoil, and plunge nations into deadly conflict. Thus evil perennially confounds our noblest efforts to achieve righteousness, nobility of character, and holiness in this life. For proof we need only to turn and examine every tribe, state, and nation on the face of the earth, including our own.

The Bible tells us that we are sinners, and that if we say we have no sin, we deceive ourselves and the truth is not in us.[4] It also says our sins were all borne away at Calvary, and our redemption was paid for by the blood of Jesus. Yet even though the burden of our guilt was lifted at the cross, and Jesus Christ covered us over with His banner of love, we still remain at best very imperfect specimens of what God had in mind. The closer we get to the Light, the more we see our defects.

Speaking personally, I confess my own transgressions to God daily. Something is obviously lacking in my mortal soul. I pray with John Donne:

> Wilt thou forgive those sins through which I run
> And do them still, though still I do deplore?[5]

But there is one other fact to remember: God knows those of us who love Him. He is aware of our dilemma. He also recognizes our sincere—albeit imperfect—desire to do His will. He accepted and still accepts our allegiance. When we come to Him afresh with broken and contrite hearts, He is faithful and just to forgive us and to cleanse us. The moral change in the universe that occurred when we gave ourselves into His keeping has not changed. It still stands. We are in His care. He has not taken His hand away.

All this is found in the Bible, and helps to make it the most unique and wonderful Book in the world. It invites us to taste its goodness, its milk and honey and its solid food. It welcomes us to feel the saving and healing power of Christ in our mind, body, and spirit. Paul says in his letter to the Philippians that he is not depending on his own righteousness to win his way to glory; rather he is depending on the righteousness "which is of God through faith." He is not perfected, but he presses on "for the upward call of God in Christ Jesus."[6]

And what does all this have to do with joy, the subject of our chapter? You will soon learn, for I am asking you to undertake a most unusual fun task. I would like you to do a little surfing through the Bible on your own, looking for joy. What a wealth of joyful expression! There is Nehemiah's classic statement: "The joy of the LORD is your strength" (8:10). The Psalms are spilling over with gladness at the goodness of God. Isaiah the prophet sparkles with joy. You will find at least 542 references to joy between Genesis and Revelation and at least 105 in the Psalms alone!

In chapter after chapter, Psalm after Psalm, and Proverb after Proverb of this ancient but so-modern Book you will find pearls and sapphires that will fill you with gladness of heart. For example:

> A merry heart makes a cheerful countenance.
> A merry heart does good, like medicine.
> A man has joy by the answer of his mouth.
> God gives wisdom and knowledge and joy to a man
>   who is good in His sight.
> The kingdom of God is not food and drink, but righ-
>   teousness and peace and joy in the Holy Spirit.[7]

The list goes on and on.

Here is one superb example of the joy the Bible contains. It is a messianic passage in the book of the prophet Isaiah. Our Lord Himself quoted it during His return home to Nazareth:

> The Spirit of the Lord God is upon me,
> because the LORD has anointed Me
> to preach good tidings to the poor;
> He has sent Me to heal the brokenhearted,
> to proclaim liberty to the captives,
> and the opening of the prison to those who are bound . . .
> to comfort all who mourn,
> to console those who mourn in Zion,
> to give them beauty for ashes,
> the oil of joy for mourning,
> the garment of praise for the spirit of heaviness;
> that they may be called trees of righteousness,
> the planting of the LORD,
> that He may be glorified.[8]

As for the New Testament, it is a-dazzle with the joy of the Lord. You will find people laughing, skipping, leaping, shouting, singing, dancing, playing instruments, celebrating. There was joy at Jesus' resurrection and joy at His ascension. Everything Paul the apostle did he seems to have done with joy. Then why don't we see it emphasized in Christian liturgy and literature, instead of the opposite?

James S. Stewart, my beloved teacher at Edinburgh University, said, "Don't be put off by these gloomy caricatures of Christianity. For God's sake don't judge Jesus, the King of joy, by them! Try the real thing, not that miserable parody of the reality. Make friends with Jesus, stand where Peter and John and Andrew did and look into His eyes, listen to the music of His voice, answer His challenge, rise and follow."[9]

What is the Bible's ultimate purpose? To bring exhilaration and delight to you and me? No. It is to bring us back to God. The One who made us who wants us back in fellowship with Him. He has something in mind for us to do. The Bible is a love letter to the whole world, but it starts with the person who opens it and reads it. It is the message of a Father pleading with His children. It is not some strange vibration out of the cosmos, nor is it a mystical distillation from the zodiac. Its purport is, "Come home, son. Come home, daughter." And it ends with the promise of the Holy Spirit that He will stay with us, will never decamp in rough terrain, and will bring us at our journey's end back to the loving Father who made us and the Jesus who saved us.

Here is where the joy enters: That welcoming party will be accompanied by a joy so exquisite in richness that nothing in earth or heaven can compare with it. "For God so loved the world that He gave His only begotten Son, that whoever believes in Him should not perish but have everlasting life."[10]

NINE

Still Waters

A book of verses underneath the bough,
A jug of wine, a loaf of bread, and thou. . . .[1]

❧

THERE IT IS, LADIES AND GENTLEMEN, a classic expression of worldly daydreaming, a portrait of alcoholic bliss by a Persian poet, astronomer, and mathematician who died nearly a thousand years ago. His name was Omar Khayyam, and his clever, satirical verses (rendered in quatrains by the Englishman Edward FitzGerald) summed up what he thought was the best of a sorry life on a sorry earth. The "best" was the satisfying grain of the field, the stimulus of the grape, and the sensual satisfaction of an attractive female companion. As for the "book of verses," it was only to waste time. The poems could be anybody's—even Omar's own.

Since Omar died in A.D. 1128, another millennium has almost passed away, and in a sense nothing has changed. Today's American culture, having virtually "emancipated" itself from its Christian roots, finds that in his *Rubaiyat*, Omar has said it all, contemporaneously and charmingly. He called it "a jug of wine, a loaf of bread, and thou," which being interpreted is food, drink, sex. Today it would be a bottle of vodka, a cheeseburger with fries, and an R-rated movie. No doubt Omar would have

71

adapted quickly to such a prospective treat in our new third millennium culture.

All this tawdry worldliness is a million miles from what Jesus meant by "My joy," which is "deeper than the honeywell, deep in the deepest flower in June." Jesus' joy is derived in all its warmth and ebullience from His Father, El Shaddai, the Lord God Almighty, the God of Abraham, Issac, and Jacob, the God of the universe and our God.

Unless we understand the true, original character of God, we will never fully feel, let alone understand, the joy of His salvation. We may accept the Bible as truth, we may commit ourselves formally to belief in God, as many have, without realizing that He wants us not just to believe in and worship Him, but to enjoy Him intimately as a child enjoys his father. God did not create the human race in order to become its Judge; rather He created it in order to become its Father. He wants us to be His own family, for His personal interest and delight.

That's the way it all started. God did not invent murder, He invented kindness. He did not invent cruelty, He invented gentleness. He gave us faces, not to scowl and bite, but to greet each other with smiles of friendship and embraces of love. He gave us voices, not to curse and scream at one another, but to speak truthfully and compassionately as our Savior did. He gave us hands, not to punch and strangle each other, but to greet and caress and help each other. He gave us feet, not to kick each other, but to walk in love and companionship with each other.

In other words, God designed us specifically to love Him and one another, and to function on that love. What the Bible says about wrath and judgment is not based on God's doings at all, but on God's reaction to *our* doings. When we violate His commandments, we can expect consequences.

Why do Christian artists always represent God with a stern expression? Why did Michelangelo paint God wearing a frown? Let me rephrase the question: Do you think God wears a smile on His face? Nowhere in any English versions of the Bible are there references to God smiling. Nowhere? Wait, there is one: the Moffatt Bible, translated from the original languages early in the twentieth century by the Scottish scholar James Moffatt (1870-1944). It contains no less than eight separate verses of the Old Testament in which God smiles. Here are some of them:

> Smile on thy servant, in thy love succor me.
> How precious is thy love, O God . . . in thy smile we
>   have the light of life.
> O God, bless us with thy favor, may thy face smile on us.
> O God of hosts, restore us to power; a smile of thy
>   favor, and we are saved!
> Smile on thy servant, teach thy laws to me.[2]

What Dr. Moffatt did was to take the several references to God's "shining face" in the King James Bible and turn them into smiles. And why not?

When Jesus stood on the Mount of Transfiguration, the account in Matthew states that His face "shone like the sun."[3] Is it possible that He too was smiling?

Thinking about God smiling makes us realize that the joy of the Lord, the subject of this book, can never be fully expressed by words. The best words can do is create a metaphor and portray an idea for the reader.

So let us go to everyone's favorite psalm, the 23rd, and examine the phrase, "He leads me beside the still waters; He restores my soul."[4] Picture in your mind a deep inviting pool, fed by a stream not far from the road of life we all travel.

Jesus brought you here. It is His own pool, and He welcomes you because He wants His joy to be in you, that your own joy might be full. It is not a therapeutic pool as such, even though it will restore your soul. It not a baptismal pool as such, though baptism is of course available. It is not intended as a sacred rite of purification or lustration such as some religions devise. It is not even a refuge or place of consolation with soporific effects.

It is just a pure foundation of sheer joy, and as you drink from it and swim and splash in it, you will find the "still waters" to be an unparalleled place of delights.

This body of water comes close to the secret that Gilbert Chesterton sensed was a part of the Person of Jesus while He was on earth—an enigmatic quality he thought was mirth, but which I am suggesting is something deeper. Its quiet sparkle is so delicious that it will make the soul quiver with joy. For the believer to bathe in it is to find life charming in its simplicity, quite apart from such embellishments and drugs as the world would like to introduce.

The lush trees and flowers bordering the pool, the leaves and petals rippling in a cool breeze, seem to augur something like a paradise beyond this planet. It is what many seek and few find, the ecstasy of tasting and knowing Jesus. In the still waters of Psalm 23 we, as part of His flock, sense the presence of God, the God of love and faith and hope, smiling on us. Goodness and mercy are everywhere. We feel them, we hear them, we taste them in the air and in the water. It is truly a time of restoring souls. Our sensibilities tell us that everything is right with God and ourselves, and our first reaction is, "Glory!"

However, the pool is surrounded by impassible briars, manzanita, and chaparral. The way to it from the main road is a secret route, a narrow path. That is to say, the path itself is a key word that takes one safely through the surrounding underbrush. The word is "Jesus," a Name that offends many. Nevertheless it is one which, accepted by the mind and heart of the believer, quickly leads past all obstacles to the quiet edge of still waters.

In seeking the pool, many travelers lose their way, for there are bypaths. Often it is because they cannot accept something difficult in the New Testament, or they are overwhelmed by the warnings in the Old Testament. They follow signs that promise shortcuts, an easier way through the thick briars, a path that does not require faith or repentance or blood atonement for sin.

So people leave the road to wander through the dense terrain, some of them bewildered, others determined and confident. Many train themselves to be almost satisfied with little, so they retrace their steps to the road and give up trying to reach the shore of God's pool of joy. You meet these people at various stopping points. They feel they have made their adjustment.

They write books about their achievements, for they consider that they have been victorious in the struggles of life; but the quintessential elixir is missing. They were caught in the thickets and gave up trying to find their way to the pool. Quite naturally, they conclude that there is no pool; but there is. It is a wonderful part of the journey.

This book will not take you to the pool. Only God's Word (the Living Water) can do that, in the power of His Spirit. But maybe—just maybe—as you read these pages you will find yourself being led to call upon the Name of Jesus and take the plunge into that delectable, refreshing pool. With Jesus it is easy to find the Still Waters where the Shepherd restores the soul. Then you will know what joy is—overwhelming, thrilling, exulting joy—for you will have it. You yourself will possess what King Arthur's Knights of the Round Table were singing about at the royal wedding in Tennyson's *Idylls of the King*:

> The King will follow Christ, and we the King
> In whom high God hath breathed a secret thing.[5]

When Christ is formed in you, the "secret thing" will be yours forever, and you will come alive, and follow Him, and know a deep peace, and hear the infectious laughter of angels.

Listen again to this Scripture:

> The LORD your God is with you,
>   he is mighty to save.
> He will take great delight in you,
>   he will quiet you with his love,
>   he will rejoice over you with singing.[6]

Imagine! Zephaniah the prophet tells of God singing over a sinner who has come out of the darkness into the Light of Life, into the joy of eternal salvation with its forgiveness and healing balm.

This book will try to tell you something about the unspeakable joy of God's love. It will also say more about Jesus, who He is and what He can do for you. It will tell you some stories about what He has done for others. And now, because of the world-wide interest in the Olympic Games that peaks every two years, the next chapter will illustrate how the joy of the Lord captured not just a town, but a whole county in the western part of the State of Wisconsin.

TEN

Gold Without Tarnish

Joy is the echo of God's life within us.

—JOSEPH MARMION

∾

IN THE WORDS OF BEN PETERSON, the tiny town of Comstock, Wisconsin, with a population of about 80, had "gone bananas." Two of the town's young men, John and Ben Peterson, ages 24 and 22, had competed in the Twentieth Olympiad in Munich, Germany, in 1972 and had come home with a silver and gold medal respectively. They were Christians.

In Chicago I watched when General Douglas MacArthur was honored with a ticker-tape parade after coming home in 1951 from the wars in the Orient. In Washington D.C. I watched as President Eisenhower was welcomed back from an unhappy meeting in 1960 with Khrushchev and the Soviets in Paris. In San Diego I watched when some of our civilian hostages were welcomed home from Iran in 1981 with helicopters and a forest of yellow ribbons, after spending 444 days in a Tehran prison.

But never did I witness such a heartwarming surge of sheer joy and ebullience among the American people as when John and Ben Peterson came home to Comstock.[1] I saw it as a fore-taste of what every lover of Jesus Christ will receive when being ushered by faith through the jewel-studded portals of heaven.

John had won the Olympic Games silver medal by placing second in the 180.5-pound class freestyle wrestling competition, defeating Horst Stottmeister of East Germany. His brother Ben was awarded the Olympic gold medal for winning the 198-class freestyle wrestling competition, defeating Roussi Petrov of Bulgaria.

When the word was flashed across the Atlantic to rural Wisconsin that Barron County had two new world champions, the citizenry reacted with astonishment and delight, then quickly leaped into action. Neighbors and fellow church-members linked together a motorcade that took the grinning athletes through four wildly-cheering nearby towns (Clear Lake, Turtle Lake, Cumberland, and Comstock).

Having no proper meeting place in which to celebrate, the Comstock citizens cut and baled the hay in Farmer Stanley Jurgenson's alfalfa field, then stored it. In the middle of his field they put up a tent and erected a lighted platform with public address system. Everyone was invited to the celebration, and cars and buses were soon rolling in from nearby counties and from Saint Paul and Minneapolis, Minnesota.

Four thousand people showed up at Jurgenson's field for an evening of cheers and joy. The Governor of Wisconsin, the Honorable Patrick J. Lucey, was there, a high school girl sang, the high school band played, and the school wrestling coach spoke. The regional director of the Fellowship of Christian Athletes told the crowd, "Silver and gold medals will tarnish, but the Bible says that when we follow Jesus Christ we are given a prize that will never fade away."

It was almost an evangelistic service. The two returning champions addressed the crowd, and each gave heartwarming acknowledgments to God, to Jesus Christ, to their parents and their church and friends. Their father, Paul Peterson, said, "I thank God for giving our boys to Esther and me, and for the privilege of pointing them to the Savior." Their pastor, Donald Toney, said, "How I thank God for people such as these!" Their mother, sister, and three other brothers were also present on the platform.

This joyful scene is recaptured for you because, as I said, it is a true parable of someone coming to Jesus Christ. Did Comstock go "bananas" over the Olympic victory of two of the town's boys? Excuse the expression if I point out that according to the fifteenth chapter of Luke the angels also went "bananas" over a sinner repenting and coming to God. What's to keep us (who aren't angels) from doing the same thing today? Let the churchbells ring with the joy of salvation!

The apostle Paul once used the athletic competition of the ancient Olympic Games in Greece to describe the Christian life. "In a race everyone who competes goes into strict training," he wrote. "They all run, but only one gets the prize."[2] As editor of *Decision* magazine I was invited to Comstock for the Peterson brothers' welcome, and I learned something about the kind of young Christian citizens the State of Wisconsin produces, and also about the prize that the Bible calls salvation.

John and Ben Peterson were far from being champions when they went to Munich. They went as unknown wrestling contenders. In speaking to the crowd at the celebration, Ben told of his lack of confidence before he came to faith in Christ. We Christians were all far from being champions before we confessed our faith in Christ. We were unknown contenders, and, as we now realize, losers. When the Petersons reached Munich no one knew them, but God knew them. John told the crowd in Jurgensen's field, "I did not go to Munich to win a medal. I went to tell the other athletes about Jesus." God honored such confidence with victory, and the people of Wisconsin recognized it. They saw that more was involved in these two young men than a couple of medals for wrestling.

The Petersons faced tough competition in their event at the Olympic Games—the toughest in the world. Today, when a person decides to seek God, the tough competition comes mostly from oneself. It's hard to face the truth that we are all sinners. It's hard to look at ourselves and admit that our mistakes and shortcomings are symptoms of something deeper: That we are living without God. Even when material successes come to us, it is a mixed advantage, for we always dissatisfied and want more. Life seems to offer an enticing but impossible dream.

I find many of my peers nearing the end of their days quietly despondent, wondering how they missed·out. There was no plat-form ceremony for them. In their ruminations they try to see what they did wrong that resulted in failure to realize their hopes. Not often do they conclude that the problem was their own sin. When the Holy Spirit begins to work in our lives, the first thing we discover is our need to repent. We learn that nothing really works for the sinner. A person can win a hundred medals, or cor-ner the gold market, or become king of the whole world, but God will see to it that his hopes fade into oblivion and his joy will turn ultimately to frustration and disappointment. That is sin's payoff in this world; or as people say, *that's life*.

There is no limit to the devastation sin can create. We hear of terrible things happening today, but in chapter 28 of the book of Deuteronomy God issues the warning of a possible curse so horrible that even in today's jaded environment it is shocking.

As sinners we find it extremely difficult to accept what Jesus offers, even when we find that nothing else works for us. That is why so often when we come to Him we come in tears—despairing, wrestling with ourselves, and losing.

But then when we confess our sin and ask Jesus to help us turn from it, He touches us and says, "Be of good cheer." He says, "Your sins are forgiven and your faith has made you whole; welcome to the kingdom of God." Yes! Us! Could anyone believe it? To our amazement, Jesus invites us as it were to the podium, hands us a gold medal and says one word: "Joy!"

Stunned and tearful, we turn away, unable to accept or even grasp what has happened. We are too conscious of our unwor-thiness. It's hard for a sinner to accept the grace of God when he knows he doesn't deserve it. After all, we haven't done any-thing—just repented. It seems to us that Jesus' medal should have been awarded to someone else.

Then, like the two Wisconsin wrestlers, we come home to find Christians greeting us, waving banners, tooting horns, wel-coming us, and celebrating with shouts and laughter and a parade. Then the congregation resounds with applause, and there are bands playing and singing and speeches and the preaching of the gospel. Angels lean over the balustrades of heaven and shout glory to God. Joy! Joy! *That is the joy of salvation!*

Is such festivity happening in your church? If not, why not make it happen? Pray! Call a meeting! Turn a baptism into a festival! That is how the joy of the Lord fits into the Christian life. Joy is not the goal; the kingdom is the goal. Joy is not the blessing; love is the blessing. But after the transformation of a human soul, the joy comes as an extra gift of heaven and a fruit of the Holy Spirit.

How do I know it's true? Because it is in God's Word. Jesus said, "These things have I spoken to you that My joy may remain in you, and that your joy may be full."[3] And I know for another reason—because it happened to me.

~~~~

Good Times, Bad Times

ELEVEN

Will Moves Through Desire

Paul Claudel, the French poet, said after listening to Beethoven's Fifth Symphony that he knew now that at the heart of the universe there is joy.

—GERALD KENNEDY

∾

"Thy kingdom come, thy will be done. . . ."[1]

Back in the 1930s, 40s, and 50s, everyone knew those words as part of the Lord's Prayer. They were recited daily in public schools, often at graduations and civic gatherings, and on Sundays in churches. Today many people consider the Old English words archaic, so let us adopt the current vocabulary.

"Your will be done." What does it mean? And what does it have to do with joy, the subject of this book?

Look at the word "will." The original word in the Greek text is *thelema*, and it is sometimes rendered "pleasure," as in Revelation 4:11 KJV. A similar word *thelesis* (translated "will") appears in Hebrews 2:4. In the Septuagint the same word *thelesis* means "good pleasure," "delight," and even "sweetness."

By this time it may appear that there are different meanings to the word "will." When we take up the subject of God's will it requires further study.

Stephen Vincent Benét wrote a poetic description of President Abraham Lincoln's wrestling with the subject of God's will during the Civil War, after some clergymen called on him in the Oval Office. Here is the way Benét imagined Lincoln's reaction to their visit:

> They come to me and talk about God's will . . .
> Day after day . . .
>   . . . all of them are sure they know God's will.
> I am the only man who does not know it.
> And yet, if it is probable that God
> Should, and so very clearly, state His will
> To others, on a point of my own duty,
> It might be thought He would reveal it me
> Directly, more especially as I
> So earnestly desire to know His will.[2]

That sounds like honest Abe. How many mistakes have been made by Christians who have imagined that they understood God's will and knew exactly what God wanted them (and others) to do!

In A.D. 1095 Pope Urban II launched a crusade to "rescue the Holy City of Jerusalem" from the Muslims or, as they were then called, "infidels." He told a huge crowd at a synod gathered at Clermont, France, *"Deus vult! God wills it!"* The crowd roared back its approval, *"Deus vult!"* but His Holiness couldn't have been more wrong. Hundreds of thousands of Europeans and Turkish citizens lost their lives as a result in an utterly wasted cause. The Muslims survived four such crusades and still retained the Holy City. The lasting result: They have hated Christians ever since.

That wise and worthy Christian, John Wesley, was convinced he could discern God's will by the "casting of lots," as was done occasionally in Scripture. Wesley was wrong. Had he had his way, the American colonies would never have known the blessing of the "Great Awakening" under the preaching of George Whitefield. Thousands of men, women, and children from

Georgia to New England were saved. Wesley informed Whitefield that he had "cast the lot" about him and it said Whitefield should not leave Britain for America. But Whitefield quietly ignored him and sailed from London to Savannah anyway. Praise the Lord!

After a new believer comes to Christ, he or she probably begins thinking, "I wonder what God's will is for my life." It's a complicated question, because insurance people think in terms of "acts of God," and others simply think "what happens" is God's will. But God is more than "fate," and His will is more than *que sera sera*. A fine New England scholar, Timothy Dwight, once pointed out, "To say God wills a thing because He wills it is to speak without meaning."[3] If I carelessly swing my car to the wrong side of the median and collide with another car, that is hardly God's will. Let's not call fatalism what is merely criminal recklessness.

It seems clear that the word "will" means in the Bible more than simply "intent" or "purpose" or "notion." Jesus placed strong emphasis on "*doing* the will of My Father." In Sunday schools the traditional interpretation of God's will has always been moral, as in "duty." That still leaves unclear the meaning of the word "will." How would it apply to God's gifts?

Aristotle once said, "*Will moves through desire.*" The thought has merit. "Will" is a much stronger word than "purpose" or "intention." When a bride tells the minister "*I will!*" in answer to his question, it carries an emphatic sound that "I intend" cannot match. Perhaps what she is saying, with all the urgency of her love, is "*I desire!*"

Let's apply Aristotle's statement to the verse in the Lord's Prayer with which we began: "Your will be done." We now read it as "Your desire be done." Instead of engaging in endless theological and philosophical discussions as to the nature and interpretation of God's will, let us simply ask, "What is God's desire?"

The first thing we notice is that whatever God's desire is on earth, it is (according to Jesus) the same as it is in heaven. And heaven, according to the Bible, is a place of everlasting joy.

Need I say more?

We need to be reminded that our Heavenly Father is a God of love and that He is neither inflexible nor arbitrary. Millions of Christians will testify that God certainly responds to prayer. Let's look again at that verse in Revelation 4:11. In the NIV it reads, "You created all things, and by your will they were created and have their being." Here the words "your pleasure" in the KJV have been changed in the NIV to "your will." Which is right? They are both right! What we will (that is, what we want) is what gives us pleasure. Everybody knows that. Some call it joy. Others call it happiness, pleasure, or fun. It has always been an aim of the human race.

If joy is what God desires for us, what does that tell us about God? It tells us He is a God of love. He is not interested in making us suffer. He does not want us to spend our lives trying to survive under conditions of near-slavery, or to waste our talents in squeezing money out of other people without producing anything useful. It is obvious that God created us so that He might enjoy us, and that raises a crucial question: Are our lives pleasing Him?

God gave us songs, and smiles, and laughter. He gave us the gift of love, so that we would help each other. He gave us sunshine and rain and beautiful growing things. I believe He tipped our planet's orbit at an angle of 23+ degrees from the equator so we could enjoy summer and winter, springtime and harvest.

Now what is it that we really want in life? We can mention jobs and houses and cars and boats and spouses and children and fixed incomes. We can discuss health and security and entitlements, and a hundred other things. We can think about fame and notoriety and adventure and achievements and wardrobes and jewelry and travel, and yet all of these remain outside the heart of what we really want.

What we all want is love and the joy it brings with it.

But here is where true Christians differ from others: It is more than simply human joy we are seeking; *we want the secret of God's love and God's joy*. And even this needs to be looked at carefully, because ultimately, as C.S. Lewis once said, it is not so much *the joy of the Lord* we are seeking as *the Lord of Joy Himself*.[4]

Speaking for myself, I want God! I want to see the bunting of Heaven, to experience the full ecstasy of the deliverance from my sins at the cross of Jesus Christ, to feel the elation of victory over the devil and all his motley crew. It's not enough to hear what wonderful things God has done for someone else. Certainly I enjoy hearing about it, but I also want those things for myself. I want to be filled with the Spirit, to sing and dance for joy, to join up with the saints in the halls of heaven as they pass by the throne, and to sing a song of triumph with them. I want to express my love for our wonderful Lord right here on earth, and I really don't know how to very well. But now I see at last that this is God's will for me. Like the apostle Paul, I have not arrived there yet, but at least it is exciting to study the road map.

How about you?

When you sit quietly in church worshiping God (or thinking about the football game that has already started), do you have an idea how much God loves you? Are you aware of the strength there is in the radiant joy of the Lord? It is like nothing else on the face of the earth.

Oh, yes, sin is also powerful. The devil came to earth bringing his diabolical baggage of misery, brutality, and despair. But that was not in the original script of creation. Don't ask me the details right at this juncture, but just thank God that He so loved the world that He set out to cancel sin and rescue us. Jesus came to us on a mission of mercy with the promise of life that is really living. He went to the cross for the joy that was set before Him, according to Hebrews 12:2, and He is now enjoying the delights of heaven.

What then is the will of God? That we should desire God! Don't desire happiness, for its staying power is weak. Don't even desire joy itself, but instead *desire Him who is joy.* Desire Him, long for Him, yearn for Him. When you have found Him, delight in Him and He will give you the desires of your heart.

That is the will of God for us on earth, as it is in heaven.

Don't miss it.

TWELVE

When God Shouts

It's better to shout than to doubt,
It's better to rise than to fall,
It's better to let the glory out
Than to have no glory at all.

—EARLY STUDENT VOLUNTEERS, ENGLAND

∽

IN 80 YEARS I HAVE NEVER read a word of commentary about the shouts in the Bible. Shouting is not normally a part of contemporary worship. In fact, it is considered out of place in church, as in polite society. I certainly don't want people shouting at me. Do you? Nevertheless if we are to consider expressions of Christian joy, we cannot ignore the shout.

My wife Ruth is anything but a shouter. Quiet and demure, she expresses her witness to Christ firmly, but in characteristically gentle tones. Shouting is not her cup of tea. She would rather be somewhere else, and so would I.

Yet the Bible tells us that God Almighty expressed Himself with shouts, and so did His Son Jesus. And whether we like it or not, many believers have found through the centuries that at times the joy of the Lord becomes so exhilarating that the only way they can express it is with a shout.

A shout of joy can take different forms of utterance. It can be a song sung loudly, an acclamation or a proclamation, or simply an ecstatic crying out. "Hosanna!" and "Hallelujah!" were expressed as shouts in the Bible. They are occasionally heard in conventional worship services today, but usually in hymns and songs. I take as a model the apostle Paul, who added one of the greatest New Testament books to the Bible when he wrote to the Christians of Galatia. In it he asked this loaded question: "What has happened to all your joy?"[1]

At the close of the book of Psalms a shout of joy is raised that is worth repeating. It is found in Psalm 150:

> Praise the Lord! . . .
> Praise him with the sounding of the trumpet,
> Praise him with the harp and lyre,
> Praise him with tambourine and dancing,
> Praise him with the strings and flute,
> Praise him with the clash of cymbals,
> Praise him with resounding cymbals.
> Let everything that has breath praise the Lord.
> Praise the Lord! (NIV)

The hundredth Psalm explains the reason for all the loudness:

> *Make a joyful shout to the* LORD, all you lands!
> Serve the Lord with gladness;
> Come before His presence with singing . . .
> *For the* LORD *is good;*
> His mercy is everlasting,
> And His truth endures to all generations.

In other words, there come times when due to the goodness of Almighty God the joy-filled believer simply has to burst forth in noisy exuberance! The next few pages seek to show why the joy of the Lord occasionally gets so exhilarating that it simply cannot contain itself.

Astronomers and cosmologists have discussed at length the possibility of the universe originating with a "big bang." One such theory contends that the universe was created by the explosion of a mass of hydrogen atoms and is still expanding. Such an ancient explosion presumably sent a spangle of stars and nebulae spinning in every direction. The "big bang" theory is now commonly taught in public schools, though no one has yet explained satisfactorily who or what it was that set off the bang. Nor have they told us what was there before the explosion.

Following that theory, some Darwinian adherents teach that a pool of slime on planet Earth started the chain of evolution; and thanks to some improbable configurations and chance fluctuations in the course of time, here we are!

It reminds me of a limerick that goes:

> There once was a brainy baboon
> Who always breathed down a bassoon,
>   For he said, "It appears
>   that in billions of years
> I shall certainly hit on a tune."

It is hard for Christians to take evolutionism seriously because its adherents are always changing their premises. The Bible teaches that the beginning of all things was not an explosion of stars as such, but rather it was the proclamation of a Word. That Word was in the beginning with God, and the Word was God.

Just how the Word was first proclaimed the Bible does not say, but it does say that "the morning stars sang together, and all the sons of God shouted for joy."[2] From that verse in the book of Job we can gather that there was some shouting going on somewhere. It charms the mind to think that God Himself, the Great Ruler of heaven, could have suddenly started the creation not with a Big Bang so much as a Big Shout! That is to say, God spoke in His holiness and the universe began, and was, and is.

A strange expression is found in Psalm 47, which describes a magnificent Israelite victory that was being celebrated with great jubilation. It seems people were clapping their hands and exalting the Lord Most High. Then in verse 5 we hear the psalmist saying, "*God has gone up with a shout,* the LORD with the sound of a trumpet."[3] How amazing! Imagine God shouting for joy! Yet there it is, in the divine record.

As might be expected, commentators are quick to explain away the verse. They say it was not God who shouted, but that the "shout" was the Jewish people's own glad cry of victory over some enemy, which they accompanied with the sound of trumpets and songs of praise.

Well, it is certainly true that shouting was frequently heard in Israel's military history. The shouts of the troops and the blowing of horns, recorded in Joshua 6, brought down the walls of Jericho. But if in Psalm 47 it was the army of Israel rather than God that "went up with a shout," I ask, why didn't the psalmist say so? Why did he say God did it? Why didn't he write instead, "The people have gone up with a shout"?

If it was really God who "went up with a shout," what does that mean to you and me? We are not thinking about some imaginary deity now, we are thinking about our Maker. Did He shout or didn't He? If He did, is He acting like us? For an answer, I turn to Genesis 1 and find God saying, "Let Us make man in Our image, according to Our likeness." So the answer is *No;* when God shouts in exultation, as He does in Psalm 47, He is not acting like us, but just the opposite: When we shout for joy we are acting like Him!

The Bible has some important things to say about shouting that are not often discussed in church; and because this is a book about joy, we intend to look at them.

Not always in the Bible did God shout joyfully. In the book of Amos the Almighty roared forth from Mount Zion. In Jeremiah He roared from on high "against all who live on the earth." In Ezekiel His voice was like the sound of many waters, and again like the sound of the wings of the cherubim. In Exodus God spoke out of a bush, in Matthew out of a cloud. In Revelation John wrote that His voice sounded like thunder.[4]

But as I read the Bible I gain the impression that the true sublime greatness of God shows forth not in His roars of indignation, but in His expressions of joy and gladness. Why?

Because joy came first! God's joy and pleasure, with love, were in the original design of God's creation and form part of the ground of reality; whereas sin and evil that appeared later are (to quote Augustine) mere corruptions of reality and goodness.

Let's look further in the Bible. In Psalm 27 the psalmist declares when trouble arises and enemies oppress him, the Lord will so protect him that his head "shall be lifted up above my enemies all around me." He then adds a curious statement: "I will therefore offer *sacrifices of joy* in His tabernacle."

Sacrifices of joy? What are they? It sounds like a nice Biblical expression, but when examined it turns out to be an apparent oxymoron. How is a sacrifice joyful? Was Abraham joyful when he tried to sacrifice Isaac? Because of my far-ranging ignorance, I was forced to consult several commentaries, and while failing to find an answer to my question, I did learn something. Joy, I was told, is not an isolated or occasional consequence of faith, it is an integral part of our whole relation to God. The joy of the Lord is something that rises above circumstances and focuses on the very character of God. I learned that there is a holy joy, so pure it exists even in the midst of sorrow. I also learned that joy comes to us from the Holy Spirit along with love, peace, and other virtues described by Paul in his letter to the Galatians.

But how do the commentators say this joy expresses itself in the Bible? Here I was really surprised. In "dancing, shouting, singing, clapping, leaping, foot-stamping, feasting and celebrating." For example, in the week-long harvest Feast of Booths or Tabernacles, the Hebrews took to the open air, living in the shade of booths made of the leafy fronds of trees. They did so in sheer gladness of heart as a way of thanksgiving, in obedience to Deuteronomy 16:15: "You shall be altogether joyful."

I learned further that after the Babylonian exile in the sixth century B.C., the great Jewish festivals lost much of their original joyous character and became solemn anniversaries. I could not help wondering, is not that also what happened to joy in the New Testament church after Pentecost? In each succeeding century the church seems to have brought in more sanctimony, solemnity, and ritual, while cutting back on the celebrating. And what do we today intend to do about it?

Still looking for an explanation of "sacrifices of joy," I telephoned Dr. Ronald Youngblood, the distinguished Old Testament scholar, author, and compiler at Bethel Seminary West. He returned the call to inform me that the Hebrew sacrifice of joy was a *shout*. As the worshiper gave his priestly offering to the Lord and the priest accepted it, the donor shouted for joy! The term "sacrifice of joy" thus really means "joyous shout!"

How does all this relate to us? How do we offer a sacrifice of joy to the Lord? I may have found an answer in the twenty-fifth chapter of Matthew. Jesus told a famous parable, implying that when His followers go out of their way to help somebody with a visit, a prayer, a gift of food, water, or clothing, they are doing it not just to help someone else, they are doing it for Jesus Himself. Thus it becomes a work acceptable to God.

Look at that again. When we do something for others that has *nothing to do with our own personal agenda*, we who love the Lord become His priests and priestesses of joy. No wonder the psalmist exclaimed, "I will sing, yea, I will sing praises unto the Lord." Yea, and shout, too, and twang the harp. To repeat, when we do it for others, we are doing it for Jesus! That's what the Lord told us, and that's what the Scripture means by a sacrifice of joy. What a beautiful concept.

We all remember the dazzling Christmas story in Luke, as he described the angels that appeared to the shepherds and shouted for joy, "Glory to God in the highest, and peace among men of His good pleasure."

Luke further tells that the voice of the Heavenly Father was heard at the baptism of Jesus: "This is my beloved Son, in whom I am well pleased." Similarly the heavenly voice was heard by Peter, James, and John on the Mount of Transfiguration (probably Tabor) saying, "This is my beloved Son. Hear Him!"[5]

On Palm Sunday a few years later, according to Luke, Jesus' disciples shouted joyously, "Blessed is the King!" as Jesus was descending from the Mount of Olives. Five days later, according to Mark's Gospel, our Lord Jesus Himself shouted twice, once in agony and once in victory. When He uttered the words "My God, my God, why have You forsaken me?" He was quoting from Psalm 22. Then at the moment of His final breath on the cross Jesus gave a shout that has always been interpreted as a signal of triumph.

Finally, according to Scripture, when Jesus Christ returns to earth He will "descend from heaven with a shout, with the voice of an archangel, and with the trumpet of God."[6]

Jesus taught that there is "joy in heaven" when a sinner repents and turns to God. He repeated it a second time: "I say to you, there is joy in the presence of the angels of God over one sinner who repents."[7] How do you imagine that joy was expressed?

The twentieth century has seen more martyrs for Christ than all the previous 19 centuries together. The time may soon come when "political correctness" or some popular New Age dogma in our own Western democracies will demand the price of Christian martyrdom. Then, as brave new gospel songs are written, we will learn all over again the meaning of the word "shout."

It inspires me to remember the young Huguenot girls in France during the sixteenth-century wars of religion, singing psalms and spiritual songs as they went to the scaffold for their faith "as gaily as they would go to the bridal couch, calling only on Christ their Savior." What a welcome they must have received in heaven!

"Shout for joy to the Lord, all the earth!" cries the psalmist. "Shout aloud. Sing for joy. Wake up, shout it aloud, don't hold back. Shout for joy, O heavens. Shout aloud, O earth beneath." And the book of Revelation ends with the Spirit and the bride calling out, "Come! Whoever is thirsty, let him come!"[8]

THIRTEEN

Silence Is Golden

A wise old bird lived in an oak;
The more he saw, the less he spoke.
The less he spoke, the more he heard—
Why can't we all be like that bird?

∾

SYDNEY SMITH ONCE SAID OF Lord Macauley, "He has occasional flashes of silence that make his conversation perfectly delightful." The gentleman's point was well taken: We talk too much.

Imagine you are standing near the edge of a huge granite mass in a high range of mountains. Before you stretches a lush valley full of native trees. A small stream splashes over the boulders below, but you cannot hear it. Everywhere is silence.

There's not a leaf that falls upon the ground,
But holds some joy of silence or of sound.

You are in a joyful, triumphal mood after your solo hike from the valley. You breathe in the mountain air deeply, and open your mouth to shout, but your voice seems reluctant to break the golden silence. You are absolutely alone. You remember how much time Jesus spent alone in silence on the mountainside with His Father. With the breeze blowing in your face you whisper, "Beautiful. Thank You, Father. Thank You, Jesus."

Giving thanks, even silently, is an easy way to open up the channels between earth and heaven. Peter Forsyth writes, "Inward joy is fulfilled in the prayer of thanksgiving."[1]

As for our Father God, with requests coming to Him every half-second from everywhere, begging, appealing, petitioning, pleading, even demanding, it must refresh His Sovereign Majesty to field a prayer that expresses nothing but gratitude. Not even an R.S.V.P.!

To be alone with silence, said Samuel Hageman, is to be alone with God. In the stillness, whether on a mountain or at home in bed, we can reflect quietly on the excellencies of Him who is always desiring to communicate with us. So we "talk" to Him with our minds and our hearts. If this is a first attempt, we tell Him, "We're sorry, but we've been thinking about starting to pray to You for a long time, but you know how it is—we just haven't got around to it." Having done that, we can relax in the silence for awhile, perhaps just contemplating the attributes of the Infinite One. If we are still on the mountain, we can look out over a distant delta and whisper with Sidney Lanier:

> As the marsh-hen secretly builds on the watery sod,
> Behold I will build me a nest on the greatness of God.[2]

Silence has always been a corridor to God. Ignatius, who was bishop of the church at Antioch some 85 years after Christ, wrote a letter to a nearby church at Philadephia and said of its bishop, "I am charmed by his sweetness of manner. He accomplishes more by his silence than others do that talk to no purpose." However, in one of the surviving manuscripts of that letter Ignatius' compliment is paid not to the bishop, but to Jesus![3] And how true it sounds.

Jesus' silent withdrawals for prayer were well-known to His disciples. Another who knew about them was Pontius Pilate. He couldn't believe his prisoner's refusal to defend Himself. Repeatedly he questioned Jesus about the charges against Him, but our Lord maintained His silence. As a Negro spiritual rendered it, "He never said a mumblin' word."

When the Welsh Revival of 1904-06 was at its height, a young miner who was one of its leaders traveled through the countryside of Wales, stopping on Sundays in villages and towns to preach in churches. The churches would be crowded, expecting him to arrive and take the pulpit. But when he showed up, he would often slip into a pew and remain there praying silently throughout while the singing and witnessing went on. Just the power of Evan Roberts' quiet presence, it was said, was electrifying. Many people were saved. It was if the congregation had a "wild surmise" of heaven itself.

A warmhearted foreign missionary, Charlie Andrews, wrote a book telling of his long years in India, during which many of his experiences were discouraging. He suffered a lot of criticism for his attitude of love toward all the Indian people. He even lost his standing in his church over a theological point. He wrote these lines:

> I have failed. Things have gone wrong, within and without, but especially within. My heart has become troubled and discouraged with the sense of repeated disappointment. Anxiety has increased. My whole inner mind has become clouded and perplexed. But He [Jesus], the great Teacher, has been bearing with my questionings as a friend, and as a friend He makes plain His own meaning, revealing His purpose.
>
> And then, ah! then, there has come silently flowing back, like the tide of the great ocean, His own boundless love into my heart, and all doubts and fears have been purged away. The dark night of the soul, with its troubled dreams, has vanished, and my eyes have been opened to the light of a new dawn. I have known once again that "His compassions fail not; they are new every morning." The very air I breathe, the sky above me, the earth at my feet—all nature now seems to be bathed in a glorious light, transfigured by the joy that is in my own soul.[4]

Peace and solitude. Absolute silence that never betrays us. As some of us enter the latter years of life, we become better acquainted with the silences, especially during the hours between sunset and sunrise. In such times of solitude our thoughts flow into memories, and we call up pleasant scenes of the past.

I am grateful to the Sunday schools I attended as a boy, and to the teachers who encouraged me to memorize different parts of the Bible, notably the Psalms. Now in my latter years, instead of picking up the worries of the day, I lie in bed at night and call up different Scriptures, thinking through them silently.

Filling the joys of silence with God's Word is a tonic not only for the human mind but also for the body. Just to be quiet! To sit among one's books hearing nothing except perhaps something pleasant in the distance, such as popcorn popping! Oliver Wendell Holmes once said, "Silence, like a poultice, comes to heal the blows of sound."[5] And what a privilege to open the Bible and read, "Wait on the LORD; be of good courage, and He shall strengthen your heart; wait, I say, on the LORD!"[6]

Here is a delightful passage that I find never fails to lift my spirit as I think my way through the verses:

> Make a joyful shout to the LORD, all you lands!
> Serve the LORD with gladness; come before His presence with singing.
> Know that the LORD, He is God. It is He who has made us, and not we ourselves;
> We are His people and the sheep of His pasture.
> Enter into His gates with thanksgiving, and into His courts with praise.
> Be thankful to Him and bless His name,
> For the LORD is good; His mercy is everlasting, and His truth endures to all generations.[7]

Notice the words *joyful, gladness, singing, thankful, bless,* and *praise*. When we keep company with such thoughts, silence becomes filled with angel sounds.

Here is another Psalm that, as one lies quietly at night, seems almost to explode with the joy of thanksgiving:

> I love the LORD, because He has heard my voice and
>   my supplications.
> Therefore I will call upon Him as long as I live.
> The pains of death encompassed me,
>   and the pangs of Sheol laid hold of me;
> I found trouble and sorrow.
> Then I called upon the Name of the LORD:
>   "O LORD, I implore You, deliver my soul!"
> Gracious is the LORD, and righteous; yes, our
>   God is merciful.
> The LORD preserves the simple; I was brought low,
>   and He saved me.
> Return to your rest, O my soul, for the LORD has
>   dealt bountifully with you.
> For you have delivered my soul from death, my eyes
>   from tears, and my feet from falling.
> I will walk before the LORD in the land of the
>   living.
> I believed, therefore I spoke: "I am greatly
>   afflicted."
> I said in my haste, "All men are liars."
> What shall I render to the LORD for all His
>   benefits toward me?
> I will take up the cup of salvation, and call
>   upon the name of the LORD.
> I will pay my vows to the LORD now, in the
>   presence of all His people.
> Precious in the sight of the LORD is the death
>   of his saints.
> O LORD, truly I am Your servant; I am Your
>   servant, and the son of Your maidservant;
> You have loosed my bonds.
> I will offer to you the sacrifice of thanksgiving,
>   and will call upon the name of the LORD.

I will pay my vows to the LORD now,
 in the presence of all His people,
 in the courts of the LORD's house,
 in the midst of You, O Jerusalem.
Praise the LORD![8]

Where Ruth and I live at present there are seven entrances into our home in addition to the front door. The seven ways are the mailbox, the telephone, the fax machine, the radio, the television set, the newspaper, and e-mail. Under such conditions a stretch of silence is not easy. The one welcome sound I prefer to all others is that of my wife's voice, which is like that of King Lear's daughter Cordelia, whose "voice was ever soft, gentle and low, an excellent thing in woman."[9]

Now I would like to take you back to the top of that granite mountain. We shall walk among the tall silent stands of yellow pine and Douglas fir, the birch and the poplar, where the woodpeckers tap, the swallows dart by, the breeze touches the treetops, and all nature seems filled with joy.

I wrote a poem once after hiking to a bit of water in the High Sierra known as "Lost Lake." Here it is:

I knelt beside a lonely lake
 where all was green and blue;
I asked the Lord to take my life
 and fashion it anew.
And as I knelt, a breath I felt
 of glory in that place;
The Spirit of the Living God
 came down in power and grace.

The wind soughed gently through the trees;
 no other sound was heard,
but as of yore Christ walked the shore
 and broke to me His Word;
and angel trumpets filled the air
 in praise to God the Son,
and all the pine trees clapped their hands
 at what the Lord had done.

Up there in the silence where God's nearness is a felt reality, it is easy to visualize Him smiling. It is easy to think of my Jesus as walking alongside us, sharing the delights of nature, but even more the blessedness of the Spirit. As the apostle Paul wrote long ago, "We look not at the things which are seen, but at the things which are not seen. For the things which are seen are temporal, but the things which are not seen are eternal."[10]

FOURTEEN

When Joy Meets Fear

Courage is fear that has said its prayers.

—KARLE WILSON BAKER

❧

THE YOUNG DRIVER WAS ON his way to Las Cruces, New Mexico, to meet his fiancée. He had no map and had lost his way, but it didn't bother him; he knew he was heading east. He was actually singing for joy when his car went off the road and into the sand on a lonely stretch of a back road in Arizona. His first panicky efforts to pull back on the road only made the tires dig in more deeply. The car was now immovable, and he had no cellular phone. For miles he had driven without seeing another vehicle. It was late afternoon, and the summer heat was almost unbearable. He had no water. He got out, locked the car, and started walking.

Five hours later the young man found himself in the darkness, still walking, with a thirst that becoming increasingly unendurable. The joy he felt at the wheel was long gone, and fear had crept into his thinking. Would he make it? Where was he? Would he die? Would they find his body by the roadside? Was he ready to die?

As he sat down and wrote a note to his parents on an identification card in his wallet, telling what had happened, tentacles of dread seemed to reach for his throat. He knew that spiritually he was not ready to meet God. His church had not prepared him. He did not want to die. He was afraid to die. He was terrified of judgment and hell. Dazed, he started on, stumbling often, for the moon was down and he was finding it difficult to stay on the road. Fearful of dying if he stopped, he kept walking all night. In the first streak of dawn he came at last upon a weatherbeaten road sign. It read:

FLAGSTAFF 25 MILES.

Exhausted, he collapsed off the pavement and began to sob.

Why should I write about fear in a book of joy? It is because of all the horrors that beset the ordinary individual in the course of a lifetime, fear is the top killjoy of them all. As the film *Titanic* dramatically illustrated, when one's ship is sinking, fear tends to crowd out all other emotions.

Turn with me to the closing chapter of the Gospel of Matthew. It opens with a scene at the empty tomb on Easter morning. Mary Magdalene and Mary the mother of James arrive to look at the body of Jesus. Just then a temblor shakes the ground. They find that an angel of the Lord has rolled the stone from the mouth of the tomb and is sitting on it. The women begin trembling with angst and fright.

The angel speaks to the women, telling them that Jesus has risen from the tomb and is going to Galilee. He invites them to look in the tomb. It is empty. Then he asks them to carry word to the disciples that Jesus is alive. Please note the next words in Matthew's text: "They departed quickly from the tomb *with fear and great joy,* and ran. . . . "[1]

So the women combined their great fear with great joy. That is different! Please look further with me at a second passage, this one in Luke 24. It is the same Easter morning scene but with slight differences. Certain Galilean women (the same ones are mentioned, with others) are at the tomb with spices and fragrant oils with which to anoint the body of Jesus. They meet two men in shining garments and are told that Jesus has risen, as He predicted He would. The women then notify the disciples.

Later the men are meeting in a room when Jesus Himself suddenly stands in the midst of them. The men are frightened—terrified—until He shows them His wounded hands and feet. The text says that then *"they still did not believe for joy."*[2] There it is again: joy in the midst of fear. Or to be more accurate: the joy of the Lord with the fear of the Lord.

In these two passages there is something the Bible is trying to tell us, and I believe it has to do with the nature of God. Over and over again the Bible praises the "fear of the Lord" as something desirable and wonderful. It is evidently not the terror that one has in encountering an angry grizzly bear, or when one is lost at night in an Arizona desert.

The fear of the Lord in the Bible is not strictly terror. It includes reverence, amazement, and awe in the presence of the Unseen. This awe, this numinous, mysterious awareness of the supernatural, as the Bible describes it, is more than a creepy or ghostly feeling. It is a warning of the presence of Majesty, and for the believer it also has a positive, uplifting sentiment, a tinge of joy in the presence of the living God. A God-fearing man or woman, then, is not a person crippled by fright, but more likely one who radiates love and even joy to a busy world.

The Bible tells us that such fear is the beginning of wisdom. "The fear of the Lord is clean . . . the fear of the Lord is strong . . . the fear of the Lord is instruction . . . the fear of the Lord is riches, and treasure, and a fountain of life." That is the way the Bible describes it. James, the brother of Jesus, begins his letter in the New Testament by advising his fellow Christians:

> Consider it pure joy, my brothers, whenever you face trials of many kinds, because you know that the testing of your faith develops perseverance. Perseverance must finish its work so that you may be mature and complete, not lacking anything (James 1:2-4 NIV).

James is telling his fellow Christians that certain kinds of fear and suffering do in fact build fiber into our souls and strengthen our characters. When we pass through such a test, we are better men and women, which is cause for joy. James is not saying that we should take delight when our worst fears are realized, or when we are actually being hurt.

Peter adopts the same tone in his first letter:

> Dear friends, do not be surprised at the painful trial you are suffering, as though something strange were happening to you. But rejoice that you participate in the sufferings of Christ, so that you may be overjoyed when his glory is revealed (1Peter 4:12,13).

Matthew says that the women knew "fear and great joy" when they saw the resurrected Christ, and Luke says the disciples "did not believe for joy." That seems to make the joy of the Lord a more wonderful concept. It fairly makes one tingle with excitement. We really are close to God!

People can easily misunderstand the expression "the fear of the Lord." They don't like the idea of fear. They protest that God is not fearsome at all—that God is love and kindness and goodness and mercy. Well, God is certainly all those things but when we take away the expression "the fear of the Lord" we have diminished the biblical concept of the holiness and greatness of God. We have also taken away some of the miraculous sheen of the joy and rapture of the Lord, the Almighty.

One human analogy I can offer is that of climbing a mountain. I will admit that just contemplating the idea of making such an ascent as Fuji, Mauna Kea, Shasta, Whitney, or Half Dome can be terrifying, particularly when one is starting out alone. The mountain is so vast, and one feels so puny. People die on such climbs! There is reason for fear, yet at the same time there is joy in the thought of scaling such an imposing height. Can I really do it? Will my body make it? Fear is present. But when after many long, arduous hours one stands on the very summit of the crag with grandeur all about, there is an exquisite, joyful sense of closeness to God unmatched perhaps at lower altitudes.

The fear of God produces joyousness like that. He challenges us to come up to the heights with Him. He dares us to test the strength that He gives us, and not just in climbing. When we realize that the fear of God is woven of the same strand as the joy of God, His love is easier to grasp, for Scripture assures us that "perfect love casts out fear."[3]

We need not be scared of the Almighty. He is fun to be with; but He is still God! Years ago I heard of a radio announcer in the old days who was asked on a call-in show if he would play the Christian recording "Jesus, Lover of My Soul." After checking he responded on the air, "We are sorry we don't have the record you requested in our studio, but instead we will play for you "My Buddy."

God is not our buddy. He might be thought of as our Daddy, our Abba Father, but not as our buddy. It is true that He is majestic and overwhelming in His might and power, and awesome in His condemnation of sin, but as His children we do not need to be timid around Him. God's true nature is love. Jesus is love incarnate. The Holy Spirit is the power and wisdom of love. Jesus did not come to earth to condemn us but to save us. Our God is a great God, a God of love and mercy and joy, not of fear and dread.

Seventy-six times from Genesis to Revelation we find the words "Fear not!" Why? Often the reason given is that "God is with us." He is the Paraclete, the One who comes alongside us to help us. He is before us, leading us. He is our rearguard, He is within us, He is nearer than our hands and feet. In fact, God is everywhere. He is omniscient, omnipotent, omnipresent, and a whole lot more.

God helps us with our human fears. When they begin to loom up in our lives to such a size that they fill us with dread, He has a resource ready for us: "Put on the armor of God! Face the enemy with the girdle of truth, the breastplate of righteousness, the shield of faith, the helmet of salvation and the sword of the Spirit, which is the Word of God!"[4] Then we can face the human fear and watch it shrink to its real size.

There is a lot to be said for some human fears, as there is for some kinds of pain. Fear can be healthy in playing a role that provides safety. Fear points out the danger zones, and makes doubly certain that our errors of judgment are corrected. Fear of failure provides the caution that tightens every bolt. Many of life's greatest achievements have been brought about by response to fears of one kind or another.

Yet in the end we must give our human fears a minus sign. They will never take home the medal or win the trophies of life. Too often they are the weapons of that accuser, the devil, and we know that Jesus Christ at the cross delivered us from the powers of darkness. It is joy—often the joy of the struggle—that provides the motive to start and complete a great work. It is joy, not fear, that teaches courage and bravery in overcoming great obstacles and eventually bringing home victory.

When I look back over my years of experience, it seems that on balance joy usually becomes the winner over fear. That is because fears and worry are so often based on things that never happen. They are vapors that vanish in the light of day. Joys, too, can be ephemeral when they are earthbound, for they often have a way of disappearing, quietly or noisily. But the joy of the Lord—there is something that will last!

The message of the Bible, then, is that joy is not blotted out by fear or adversity. It simply waits until the real cloud passes. It does not deny the existence of the cloud; it does not despise the cloud or fight it. It waits, knowing that when at long last the sky clears, the joy will shine brighter than ever.

The fearful young man lost in the Arizona desert—a friend of mine—was actually stranded on an Indian reservation. A young Indian boy came along that morning on a horse, found him, gave him water, and allowed him to ride the horse back to safety.

Fear not. God reigns!

FIFTEEN

Joy When It Hurts

To get the whole world out of bed,
And washed, and dressed, and warmed, and fed,
To work, and back to bed again,
Believe me, Saul, costs worlds of pain.

—JOHN MASEFIELD IN *THE EVERLASTING MERCY*

∽

PAIN! PHYSICAL PAIN, MENTAL PAIN, emotional pain, psychological pain, neurotic pain, imaginary pain. Sharp pain, gnawing pain, slow pain, dull pain, recurring pain, wasting pain. What can one say about it with respect to joy? We are born in pain, we live by enduring and inflicting pain, and mostly we die in pain. Today billions of people are being nagged by pain, many of them constantly. If ever there was a killjoy, its name is pain. As C.S. Lewis expressed it, "Suffering is not good in itself." It makes life miserable for deserving and undeserving.

The best way to start is always with the Bible. The prophet Micah, in a famous chapter, called on all who trust in God to "love mercy."[1] If we would follow Jesus, we must demonstrate sympathy and tenderness as He did toward those who suffer. As Lewis says, "What is good in any painful experience is, for the sufferer, his submission to the will of God, and, for the spectators, the compassion aroused and the acts of mercy to which it leads."[2]

It is said that on any given day, three-fourths of the human race isn't feeling well. Books on pain and suffering vastly outnumber the books on joy, more than one hundred to one. Many people don't want to hear about other people's pain, but they are quite willing to talk about their own. As I understand it, the general attitude toward pain developed by Americans during the past century of medical research and progress is to get rid of it as expeditiously as possible. Sympathy is always acceptable, but it's boring to spend time blaming the pain on anyone or anything. Just stop it, people tell us. Take a pill; skip fortitude and bravery. As my dentist says, "We don't make heroes around here."

Does God send pain? Is that what He is like? In recent weeks I have been reading some theological articles that set out to justify God's reasons for inflicting pain on the human race. In *The Problem of Pain*, C.S. Lewis suggests that pain is "God's megaphone." Others treat pain as "God's warning." In Psalm 119 we read:

> Before I was afflicted I went astray, but now I keep Your word. . . . It is good for me that I have been afflicted, that I may learn Your statutes. . . . I know, O Lord . . . that in faithfulness You have afflicted me.

That seems to attribute pain directly to God.

In the vast literature on the subject one learns about punitive pain, corrective pain, undeserved pain, submissive pain, and even redemptive pain. I am slow to regard pain as divine punishment, or to consider sickness an instrument of God to promote redemption. Many hold such views, but I find little in Jesus' teaching along those lines. To be candid, I am vastly ignorant on the subject, and find it singularly unattractive. Shakespeare wrote, "Sweet are the uses of adversity," but some of his platitudes don't wear well. I wonder which particular pain he had in mind when he wrote that.

Many of the common kinds of pain and suffering seem to be senseless and lacking in redeeming qualities. They afflict the just and the unjust indiscriminately. It is even harder to rationalize the suffering of a whole race, such as took place during the Holocaust, which left such a stain on the twentieth century.

My beloved late wife, Winola, was a woman of God if there ever was one, but after enduring weeks of the most extreme suffering, she died of cancer. During her last days her groans and cries of pain were heard throughout the convalescent home even after she lapsed into unconsciousness. In such cases the joy comes only as one thinks of the beloved as being with Jesus, free from pain and reveling in the everlasting fellowship of the saints in glory.

In the New Testament we find Jesus in the flesh, cheerfully walking about Galilee in excellent health, saving and healing men, women, and children, and in the process getting rid of pain. At His touch diseases were cured and evil spirits were exorcised. Those to whom Jesus ministered began jumping and leaping for joy. They shouted and sang and worshiped God.

From Jesus' example I am convinced that the Heavenly Father wants His people as He had originally created them: free, healthy, and filled with gladness of heart. Yet in the Old Testament, specifically in the book of Job, it is clear that God allowed Satan to inflict pain on a righteous man. Does He still? That's one of the questions we want explained when we get to heaven.

In the New Testament the pain that Jesus suffered on the cross was as cruel as the Romans knew how to make it; yet it was different. That pain, endured for us, became atoning and redemptive pain. By the grace of God, Jesus' suffering became a passport to our wholeness and joy. Thus the blood shed at the cross became healing for all of those who believe in His glorious resurrection from the dead.

Apart from the pain of Golgotha, then, can any pain be said to have been actually good? Yes, indeed. I leave it to the medical profession to answer such questions, but we all know that pain often tells the sufferer what and where the trouble is that causes the pain. The problem is that when the source of pain is discovered and isolated, it does not always respond to treatment. Healing, as was the case with Winola, sometimes turns out to be insoluble in this life. However, the final chapters of the book of Revelation assure us that a final solution does exist. They leave us with the joy of this assurance: that this life is not the only life.

Christians also recognize one kind of human suffering that is peculiarly honorable and good. The Bible itself links it to the joy of the Lord. That is the pain caused by the persecution of believers for the cause of Jesus Christ.

Frank Uttley writes, "Christ seemed to put persecution into a different category from sickness and disease, at times even regarding it as a means of blessing. 'Take joy,' Jesus said, 'when you are persecuted for righteousness sake, for yours is the Kingdom of Heaven.' He also told His followers that 'if they persecuted Me, they will persecute you. In the world you shall have tribulation, but be of good cheer: I have overcome the world.'"[3]

The distinction between suffering caused by persecution and other forms of suffering is significant. Pain under such duress turns a questionable "bad" into a positive "good." We regard the acute pain the apostle Stephen suffered while he was being stoned for his faith in Jesus as a badge of honor. The Christian church esteems Stephen its first martyr. John Foxe's *Book of Martyrs* is freighted with stirring stories of Christian men and women who defied pain magnificently when facing their accusers.

It is significant that in our own time the continuing persecution of Christian believers, often with torture, in dozens of countries around the world is finally gaining wider recognition. It has been said that more Christians have died for their faith in the twentieth century than in all the previous 19 centuries combined.

In his beautiful book *The Tender Touch of God*, Michael MacIntosh describes the healing process in simple but powerful terms: "Stop the bleeding, dress the wound, let God heal."[4] In so doing he drew upon some famous words of Monsieur Ambroise Pare, the famed surgeon of Agincourt (1415), now considered the father of modern surgery. Today we should be continually grateful to the armies of doctors, nurses, and aides who are committed to the reduction and alleviation of pain in our world. Never should we let the cacophany of medical politics so deafen us that we cannot see the beauty of healing that is taking place in our midst.

Meanwhile it is hard to say a good word for pain when one reads about the horrendous, painful cruelties inflicted by human beings on each other even today in many parts of the world. A drunken driver who is taken to a hospital in pain after an accident deserves his punishment, we say. But what can we say about another victim in the same hospital, an innocent child facing a life of perpetual pain as the result of a drive-by shooting?

Human pain has been around for thousands of years and seems to be on the increase in our technological age despite the painkilling drugs. No doubt the devil and his minions are busy at their forges and laboratories, inventing and devising new, repulsive, excruciating forms of human torture. That too is part of the mystery of iniquity; but in the midst of it Christians are heartened to read in the book of Revelation that a day will soon come when there will be no more crying and no more pain. Praise the Lord!

Pain does have this positive value: It will bring to a halt our indulgence in wasteful and useless thoughts, and force us to concentrate on more important matters. It can even galvanize us into action. A young boy growing up in a Christian home in Ohio had left home and was working on a canal boat when he injured his foot while chopping wood. He contracted blood poisoning and soon became an invalid. During the long, painful months in bed he resolved to seek an education upon recovery. He studied for the ministry but then became a teacher, then a school principal. During the Civil War he joined the 42nd Ohio Volunteers, became a hero during the fighting at Shiloh and Chickamauga, and rose to major general. After serving in

Congress as Representative from Ohio and U.S. Senator, he was elected President of the United States. It was while lying in bed in pain that he decided to change the direction of his life. His name was James Abram Garfield.

When in pain we can also call to mind our obligations to those we love, and accomplish tasks that we keep putting off. We can offer up prayers long unsaid and read chapters in the Bible long neglected. We can even recall friends in far worse pain than we are suffering, and make fresh contacts with them in the Lord. Thus time spent in pain can be used eventually to reorient our lives.

Pain has a way of drawing Christians to their knees in prayer. Whether one is praying for one's own needs or is interceding on behalf of others, the fact that God answers such prayers with healing has been certified and confirmed by literally millions of people. A person prays; the pain stops. Always? No, not always, but often enough to make me, for one, a firm believer in prayers for healing.

During World War II I served for a time as a military hospital chaplain, visiting the wards daily, praying with wounded soldiers just arrived at Hamilton Field from the battlefields of the South Pacific and offering them the promises of God and the sacraments of the church. Believing Christians have the highest regard and admiration for persons engaged in the professions of physical and mental healing. Yet we know also that there is a ministry beyond medication to those who are never healed. Even among them while there is life, there is hope. The Gospel of Mark describes a woman who spent all her money on physicians and whose pain only grew worse at their hands. When healing did come to her, it came from the Son of God.[5]

Recently I was surprised to read the statement, "Most of the major religions have seen pain as necessary for coming closer to God." Where, I ask, is that thought found in the Bible? Where is there any evangelical agreement to it?

My friend and late prayer partner Captain Harry Jenkins was a war hero and a cheerful, committed Christian. When he was shot down over Vietnam and then subjected to the horrors of the "Hanoi Hilton" for seven years, he proved a great encouragement to his fellow prisoners. Now I ask, was it "necessary" that Harry Jenkins sit in pain hour after hour on his torture stool "in order to come closer to God"? How absurd. The truth is that for seven years a loving God stayed close to Harry, healed him, and brought him safely home.

C.S. Lewis wrote that the Christian doctrine of suffering requires self-surrender and obedience. This means that if we can't get rid of the pain we should simply learn to endure it. After all, things could always be worse. But Lewis adds something quite interesting:[6]

> The Christian doctrine of suffering explains, I believe, a very curious fact about the world we live in. The settled happiness and security which we all desire, God withholds from us by the very nature of the world; but joy, pleasure and merriment He has scattered broadcast. We are never safe, but we have plenty of fun, and some ecstasy.

Amen! There is another important point of doctrine I would add. The comedian Flip Wilson sometimes enacted the role of a very comical young lady named "Geraldine," who explained her unusual activities by saying, "The devil made me do it." "Geraldine's" error lay not simply in acknowledging the devil as a joke, but in refusing to accept personal responsibility for her behavior.

The demonic is very much involved as a source where pain is concerned, and always has been. When a bent-over woman came to Jesus on a Sabbath day to be healed, Jesus straightened her back and healed her, bringing great joy to the woman and to those who witnessed the miracle. The synagogue leader who was present waxed indignant, but Jesus said, "Ought not this woman . . . whom Satan has bound—think of it—for eighteen years, be loosed from this bond on the Sabbath?"[7] An answer to our Lord's rhetorical question is found in 1 John: "For this purpose the Son of God was manifested, that He might destroy the works of the devil" (3:8).

We Christians sit by a loved one in pain, or receive a call from the sheriff about a loved one in trouble and hurting, and we are tempted to ask, "Why is all this happening to us? How do we explain it?" At such times it might be well to listen to "Geraldine's" demonic excuse. Satan is cruel, and he operates still in our midst, every day, every hour, every minute. If there is one resource Christians have that can discomfit the devil and disturb his machinations, it might be the subject of this book: the joy of the Lord. As Paul wrote, we are not ignorant of Satan's devices. Scoffing the scoffer is a well-tested weapon.

Finally, we have the example of Christians in pain who have used their condition to lead others to Christ.

A Christian friend of mine was arrested during a demonstration that turned violent, and wound up in a jail cell with both shoulders dislocated. While she lay on her cot in intense pain, the young woman who was her cell-mate approached her bunk, crying.

"I'm so sorry to bother you," she said, "I know you're hurting, but you see I've just got to know Jesus and get right with God. I've been horrible. Please, please tell me how to find God!"

"At that moment," my friend told me, "I knew pain, but I also knew joy."

Perhaps you are asking, "Where is the joy 'takeaway' in all this for me? Is there something I can do if I want to get in on Jesus' secret?" Yes, there is. For openers, go to a Christian bookstore and get yourself a brand-new Bible. Start reading in both the Old and New Testaments, underlining such words as joy, delight, gladness, and singing wherever you come across them.

Take special note of the last three verses of the book of the prophet Habakkuk, who was one of the greatest men of any age. He wrote at the time of Nebuchadnezzar's conquest of Jerusalem (586 B.C.), and his words apply directly to us in the 1990s:

Though the fig tree does not bud
    and there are no grapes on the vines,
though the olive crop fails
    and the fields produce no food,
though there are no sheep in the pen
    and no cattle in the stalls,
yet will I rejoice in the LORD.
    I will be joyful in God my Savior.
The Sovereign LORD is my strength;
    he makes my feet like the feet of a deer,
he enables me to go on the heights.[8]

What contentment! What deep assurance! The promise is that even when life's supports fail us, our faith in God has us walking on air—lighthearted and surefooted.

I suggest that you resolve not to dwell unduly on the one pain or problem that is giving you so much trouble. Shelve it. We were not placed here to concentrate on ourselves as some animals do, but to serve the Lord and help each other. Try echoing the words of the psalmist, who said, "Let me hear joy and gladness!"[9]

Heart's Delights

SIXTEEN

What Is Happiness?

Happiness too swiftly flies.

—THOMAS GRAY

THE TIME HAS COME TO take a careful look at "the pursuit of happiness," an expression enshrined in the American Declaration of Independence. Such "pursuit," together with "life" and "liberty," is therein declared to be an "inalienable right" that the Creator has endowed upon "all men."

For millions of us happiness is the basic fabric of the American Dream. For some it is a kind of materialistic Nirvana, featuring such attractions as sports utility vehicles and luxury cruises. But for others happiness is far more than a wisp or a vapor; it is a present fact of daily life.

As a goal of life, happiness seems hard to top. As a word it is one of the most magnificent and exciting in the English language. To remove it from our vocabulary would be a terrible loss, for the term "happy" has woven itself into our daily conversation.

We can't get away from the word. Its current meaning carries even more than the bright, pleasant feeling of gladness and delight. Thus "happy" is sometimes used to signify something good and right, in contrast to the opposite: "I am happy about the way it turned out." "A better arrangement would make them happier." "We will be happy to do this for you." Sometimes it is even worked incorrectly into a description of compulsive behavior, as when a gunman is described as being "trigger-happy" or a comic as "slap-happy."

Since our marriage in 1987 Ruth and I have known nothing but what is known as happiness in our relationship, and we know scores of Christian married couples who, if asked, could match that statement. Such testimonies appear virtually unknown to the media, mainly because "happily married" people don't talk much about their lives together. The depressing news we hear and read about daily comes from the clash of incompatible temperaments.

Happiness can be found in every segment of society, in every nation and culture, rich and poor, advanced and undeveloped. It appears that people with less money are happier than the wealthy, despite the lack of creature comforts that the gated neighborhoods find indispensable. Being poor does not prevent people from being happy, and being rich does not keep people from being miserable.

Yet when we try specifically to define the word happiness, we encounter dissension. What is it? Is it glee? Bliss? Gaiety? Elation? Definitions of the word often make it sound as if we all have a clear vision of happiness, and yet no one really knows exactly what it is.

Here is one of my favorites: "Happiness is the look on a dieter's face on reaching the desired weight and heading for a restaurant." Jean-Jacques Rousseau came up with something similar: "Happiness is a good bank account, a good cook, and good digestion." Someone has said, "Happiness is never God-given, only God-permitted." Another has said that happiness is "not getting what you want, but wanting what you get." George Bernard Shaw wrote that "a lifetime of happiness would be hell on earth," and poet Edmund Spenser believed that "here on earth is no sure happiness." Schopenhauer, the gloomy philosopher, said that happiness is "simply relief from pain."

Historians tell us that in the original wording of the American Declaration of Independence, the "inalienable rights" guaranteed by the Creator were "life, liberty, and property." When objection was made by some of the Colonial delegates, Thomas Jefferson changed the word "property" in the final draft to "the pursuit of happiness." But as the New England writer Nathaniel Hawthorne soon pointed out, "When happiness is the object of pursuit it leads us a wild-goose chase and is never attained." Everyone wants to be happy, but not many make it to Bali Hai; and when they do arrive, it turns out often that they have reached just another island.

Seeking earlier help, I went back to Aristotle (384–322 B.C.).[1] It seems this famed Greek scholar singled out happiness (*makarios*) as the "most noble and most pleasant" of all human goals, much to be preferred over ambition, duty, self-mastery, or perfection. He equated human happiness with excellence and magnificence. Splendid! But when he began to describe his great-minded, excellent, magnificent man, he lost me. Listen to this:

"He [the 'happy' man] is his own best friend, and he thinks nothing is important. He is never fired with imagination, since there is nothing great in his eyes except, of course, himself, whom he values highly. He justly estimates himself at the highest possible rate. He wishes to be superior. His contempt for others makes him a bold man. He seeks honor through virtue and excellence, and is disposed to do men service, but he is ashamed to have a service done for him."

And this prig is supposed to be happy?

The French author Blaise Pascal (1623-1662) wrote, "All men seek happiness. This is without exception. Whatever means they use, everyone tends toward this end. It is the motive of every human being, even of those who hang themselves."[2] I love Pascal. He was a Christian and a brilliant scientist. He invented the adding machine, which later developed into the computer. His "Provincial Letters" are some of the funniest pieces ever composed by an avowed believer. But when he connected happiness with the end of a noose he may perhaps have come up a byte short.

Professor William James (1842-1910), the distinguished Harvard psychologist and author of *Varieties of Religious Experience*, wrote, "If we were to ask the question, 'What is human life's chief concern?' one of the answers we would receive would be, 'It is happiness.' How to gain, how to keep, how to recover happiness is for most men the secret of all they do."[3] Unfortunately the professor failed to give us specific directions to gain, keep, and recover.

Thus happiness for our sages seems to be a distant, unobtainable yearning. It is like the mechanical rabbit that the greyhounds chase and never catch. Some say that if it exists at all it is momentary, transitory, brittle, unstable, and fickle.

Perhaps that is why most of the world's literature from Homer to Hemingway is devoted to presenting the readership not with a luscious luau of human happiness but with a "Benjamin's mess" of human woe and anguish. The literary scene sets out to show that even when the customary tools for achieving happiness (such as beauty, wealth, and power) come within human reach, the recipients find the happiness escaping and their lives filled with bitterness and regret. Either that, or they destroy themselves chasing some imaginary "Moby Dick."

As in life, so in literature. The lovely literary exceptions I would make are the nineteenth-century English novels, which always close (George Eliot's excepted) with a happy, delightful chiming of wedding bells. But novels are fiction, and most great novelists with whose work I am familiar—even humorists such as Mark Twain—seem personally to be rather surly and reclusive.

When we look up the origin of the word "happiness," we find that it is not a biblical word. It comes from an Old Norse root, "hap" or "happ." This root carried the specific meaning of "good fortune," "chance," or "luck in life." Our current words "perhaps," "mayhap," "happening," "happenstance," "haply" and "happy-go-lucky" are all derived from the same root as "happiness."

Originally, then, happiness simply meant what happens—the "luck of the draw." But that is not what people in the English-speaking world today understand. Happiness does not necessarily depend on circumstances, nor is it caused by them. "Luck" and "chance" may help to create conditions of happiness, but they are not themselves happiness.

Sigmund Freud (1856-1939), considered the father of modern psychology, made a remarkable statement in his *Introductory Lectures on Psychoanalysis*. He said, "It seems that our entire psychical activity is bent upon procuring pleasure and avoiding pain, that it is automatically regulated by the Pleasure-principle."[4] Dr. Freud was wise enough not to discuss happiness, as he was limiting his interest to nervous disorders; but it is obvious that the "Pleasure-principle" has the same goal that Thomas Jefferson had when he added "the pursuit of happiness" to the Declaration of Independence. Even neurotics want to be happy.

Socrates, the greatest of the Greek philosophers, had a friend named Aristippus, an African from Cyrene. This man seems to have reduced happiness to the dimensions of a stopwatch. He is reported to have said that happiness is simply "the pleasure of the moment—and" he added, "that's all that counts."[5]

Certainly we are happy when we complete a big assignment, or when the news is flashed that our candidate has been elected, or when the e-mail tells us that a darling baby is born. Who of us would not be happy to have a wee grandchild rush into our arms? Aristippus had something. A beautiful golf drive makes me feel great—until I slice the next shot. So when a time of happiness comes, says Aristippus, enjoy it to the full, but don't count on overtime.

When we turn at last from discussing happiness to the joy of the Lord, we find something very different. As Robert Louis Stevenson said, "To miss the joy is to miss all." It comes to us from heaven trailing clouds of glory, and flows through us to others from springs deep within our own souls. This joy is the second fruit of the Holy Spirit.

Billy Sunday once declared, "If you have no joy, there's a leak in your Christianity somewhere." Joy, the joy of the Lord, is not something that vanishes when an urgent telegram arrives or a skid takes place on an icy sidewalk. Joy is a constant. It stays and weathers the shocks of life because God also stays. At such times, where else can we turn?

Dostoevsky implied in his famous *Legend of the Grand Inquisitor* that Jesus never promised to make people happy; instead He said, "I will make you free."[6] The Inquisitor insisted that people cannot handle freedom; they prefer an organization that vanquishes freedom in order to make them happy. To those of us who have claimed Jesus as our Savior and Lord, He brought something better than happiness. He brought freedom, but He also brought joy, which joy is Himself. He is our joy. He left us these beautiful words, first given to His disciples: "These things I have spoken to you, that My joy may remain in you, and that your joy may be full" (John 15:11).

Happiness itself is still desirable. In our fallen world we need all the happiness we can get, even if it turns out to be short-lived. But it's best not to sit around waiting for it or to waste time "pursuing" it. Happiness appears often when we least expect it.

Let me continue to wish you Happy Birthday, Happy New Year, Happy Holidays, and all the other happy experiences. But there is a deeper wish in my heart: that the love of God in Christ Jesus may be poured out into your heart by the Holy Spirit, and that He will bless you with joy, true joy, wonderful joy, not today, not tomorrow, but always.

Life has its ups and its downs, its whoops and its "oops." May Jesus see that your life has quick and easy access to melody and mirth in spite of everything, for in truth, *you* are His joy.

SEVENTEEN

God's Crepe Suzettes

*Till you can sing and rejoice and delight
in God . . . you never enjoy the world.*

—THOMAS TRAHERNE

PSALM 37 IS ONE OF THE most beautiful pieces of writing the world has ever seen. It had an astonishing effect on the British nation after Winston Churchill quoted from it during the Battle of Britain in 1940. We who would find the joy of the Lord need to reflect often on those words, "Don't worry about evildoers, the Lord will take care of them." (Churchill quoted the KJV, "Fret not!")

But life must be faced every morning, and it is a fact that as the world enters a new millennium (thereby unconsciously honoring the birth of Jesus Christ), we are facing rampant new horrors worse than anything the legendary Pandora ever let out of her box.

Even so, we who are older take the long view. We carry in our heads the memories of Soviet officials who kept threatening us through the 40s and 50s and 60s and 70s with the bomb that our own traitors had stolen and given to them. We remember Stalin, Litvinov, Molotov, Vishinsky, Beria (the head of KGB), Brezhnev, and Khruschchev (the one who came to our shores and told us, "We will bury you"). How we dreaded to hear their taunts! But where are they all today? They're gone! Poof! So we thank God and take courage, and refuse to yield our serene belief in the goodness of God.

During school days I fretted because a whole lot of other fellows became athletic heroes and were admired by everybody, and I was looked on as puny and insignificant. Do you know what happened to those muscular football heroes? They're almost all dead. Even my enemies are all dead, and I'm still here. Amazing.

Look at the third verse of Psalm 37: "Trust in the LORD and do good; so shalt thou dwell in the land, and verily thou shalt be fed" (KJV). That's a word for all of us, for we ought to be good citizens. We ought to do what's right. Jesus told us to perform good works. That's what Christians are expected to do.

But that's not the secret of the Gospel's power; that's only what we are supposed to do. It's existing, not living. It's our duty to God and society. Sometimes it's not much fun, but it must be done. Somebody has to bring in the food and take out the trash.

Now look at the fourth verse: "Delight thyself also in the LORD, and he shall give thee the desires of thine heart" (KJV). That happens to be one of the most important verses in the Bible. The word "delight" means to "take joy." That is the secret goal for which most human beings are looking. That is the pearl of great price, the treasure hidden in the field.

The Bible says that we should love one another (Romans 13:8). Why should we love each other? Is it because we are lovable? No, it is because God is love.[1] He didn't create love, He *is* love. And we are to love because He told us to, and because that is the way to joy, and that is really what we all want. You can have love without joy, but you cannot have joy without love.

But this verse in Psalm 37 is careful to say that we should *delight* ourselves *in the Lord*. Why is that? Because, it says, He will then give us the desires of our hearts.

What is it that we are living for? What is the thing we want out of life that keeps us going? Is it money? Sex? Nice clothes? Travel? Relief from pain? Security? A condo? A sport utility vehicle? Is it getting even with someone who has hurt us? No, these are only means to an end. They are way stations on the road to something you really want—or think you want.

Let's keep on this track: What are the desires of our hearts? Here is what some people say: "I want so-and-so to love me. I want a staff promotion. I want to be transferred to another job. I want the money to go to college. I want a church of my own, with 80 percent tithers. I want to write a bestselling book about Jesus, and then get someone to make a movie about it. The desire of my heart is to find someone who will marry me and treat me right. The desire of my heart is for my family to love me. The desire of my heart is to do something with my life, to serve my country and my God."

But how do we go about achieving such things? It tells us right here. There's no "going about" at all. There's nothing we have to do, just "delight yourself in the Lord, and He will give you your heart's desire." Fall in love with Him. Worship Him. Talk with Him. Listen to Him. Witness to Him. He is a lovely God, and He loves you so much that He sent His Son to die for your sins on the cross of Calvary, and fit you to live with Him in the mansions of heaven.

But here's the catch. When you begin "delighting yourself in the Lord," something is going to happen to a lot of those goals that once were the "desire of your heart." It's now apparent that some winners of the Olympic gold medal are finding that with the passage of time, the gold loses its sheen. Fame is fleeting. The medals are quietly put in a canvas bag and life goes on. The same principle applies to each of us. It is called "maturity" or "growing up in all things" to "the stature of the fullness of Christ." In gradual ways God will purify and reshape some of our desires so they do not seem important any more, while other goals He gives us are marvelously and miraculously strengthened.

Not long ago a group of people who called themselves "Heaven's Gate" committed mass suicide, thinking that they would thereby ride a comet to the "next level" where they would discover the joy they couldn't find here. Wrong means, wrong end.

What is the end you are looking for? Not unlikely it is what we all want: a life filled with good health, lots of love, and freedom to act. The efforts we make to get on top of our environment (and some of us work very hard), all the money we try to save and the struggles we go through in rearing our children, all our donating to worthwhile causes—in all this, what are we actually looking for? Surely it's not pride. Not ambition. Not vengeance. Not lust. For millions of people the real end is simply joy. Yet how often we take shortcuts and employ the wrong means, and thereby lose it all! Our little flower blossoms only to "waste its fragrance on the desert air."

That's the way God made the universe. In Revelation 4:11 we find that He made creation for His own pleasure. He designed it all by clockwork. He had a plan—a plan for Himself and a plan for us—and it was all to end in joy. There must have been a smile on the Father's face when He set this particular planet in its orbit for us. He did an excellent job. Then He created a beautiful man and a beautiful woman for His own pleasure, and He put them in a garden and said, "Enjoy yourselves." Talk about a purpose in life: That was it. Hallelujah!

Well, what happened? You know what happened. You're a sinner, just like me. Our first parents were disobedient to the heavenly purpose. They got off-track because they were looking for power. "You shall be as gods! You shall have the knowledge of good and evil."[2] But that's not joy. The joy was already there, and they blew it. It's very sad, because now we have this sin problem, and our planet is obviously under a curse. And yet in the midst of all our sorrow and pain and wars, God did not forsake us. He looked down in compassion on our troubles and fears and He seems to have said, "I'm going to help these people. I'm going to send my Son down there, and He will teach them what my original purpose was in the creation." In any case He sent Jesus to be with us—His only begotten Son, whom He loved so dearly. The Father, who knows all, knew that His Son would suffer and die on our behalf, but He sent Him anyway. Thus in a way that only the Trinity can explain, it was God Himself who came.

And Jesus walked the dusty roads of earth with a smile on His face, like His Father. Do you know that God has a smile on His face? It's a shame that in our churches there are pictures and statues and icons of Jesus, but they never show Him smiling. If you go to Rio de Janeiro you will find this magnificent statue on top of the Corcovado overlooking the city. It is Christ the Redeemer with His arms outstretched, but He is not smiling. He looks so sad.

When I read my New Testament I learn that Jesus was first and foremost a Man of Joy. He said, "I have Good News. I have glad tidings of great joy." The kingdom of God is a kingdom of joy![3] That's what Jesus went around telling people, lifting their spirits by saying, "Be of good cheer! Be of good cheer!"

Wouldn't you like to have been there in Galilee? Imagine boarding a 747 and flying over to Palestine and landing there at the airport at Nazareth! Then you would walk over the hills to the Sea of Galilee, and just stand on the edge of the crowd that had gathered around a Man. And you could understand the language that He was speaking. You would ask someone, "What's going on?" And he would reply, "It's Jesus, and a few minutes ago He stopped a funeral procession, and He opened the casket and told the man to sit up." And suddenly you would hear a big shout from the people: "Another miracle!"

Then maybe you would hear a tambourine, and a drum, and then the people would begin to clap. Just suppose, while you were standing on the edge of the crowd by the seashore, that Jesus would spot you. He would said, "See that person there? I want that person to come up here. Make room, won't you?" And the whole crowd would part and you would come right up. He would reach out and take your hand, and call you by your name, the name His Father had given you. How would you feel? Would you sense an exuberance, a joy, an ecstasy, a jubilation, that the Son of God had called you? So then He and the crowd would move on and you would go with them. And you would go from place to place and Jesus would be your Friend. Isn't that what you're looking for?

He's calling you today. He's here, and He's calling your name, and He's saying, "Follow me."

Jesus came to bring us joy, among other things, and it was for future joy that He went to the cross. It's in Hebrews 12:2: "Who for the joy that was set before Him endured the cross, despising the shame, and has sat down at the right hand of the throne of God."

Not long ago I was at a radio station on a call-in program in Colorado Springs, and this young fellow called in with a curious statement. He said, "I became a Christian about a year ago, and I've been going to church, but I feel that there is a party going on, and I'm left out." Do you know what he was talking about? He was talking about the fifteenth chapter of Luke.

In that parable the young man who had been a prodigal was coming back to his father. When he came back, what did the father do? His son had taken the money that the father had given him out of his inheritance, and had wasted it. He was just a no-good kid, a beach bum or whatever. He came back and said in effect, "Father, I am no longer worthy to be your son; make me as one of your hired servants. I have wasted my substance in riotous living and I'm no good."[4]

And what did the father do? First of all, he kissed him. He met him on the road before he reached the house, and he kissed him. Then he put a robe around him, and a ring on his finger, and sandals on his feet. He brought him into the house and said, "Kill the fatted calf, we're going to have a feast." And he called for music and he called for dancing, and the Book says, "They began to be merry."[5]

Merry? Yes. That is Jesus' word. Is that a fair description of the church? E.M. Forster, the brilliant English novelist, was probably not a believer, but he has left a most unusual criticism of the church. He wrote, "Christianity has shirked the inclusion of merriment."[6] My own experience agrees with him. But why should it be so? Merriment is a part of the good life that Jesus promised us. Why should we Christians bend over backward to establish solemn reputations of dignity and gravity that so often come across as pomposity? Did our Lord go in for ceremonious taciturnity? Or did He tread this life with a light touch?

When Jesus described the father in this parable, He really meant God, didn't He? If not, why else did He tell the parable? But where did He get the idea that God would order music and merriment and dancing? There's only one place: He got it in heaven. That's what heaven is going to be like. You'd better learn how to clap your hands, because there will be a lot of rejoicing in heaven. I'm not sure what kind of merriment there will be, but there's going to be a lot of joy in heaven because that's all heaven is: joy.

But it seems the young prodigal had an older brother, and he had been working with a scythe out in the fields, and he came up to the house dripping with perspiration and said, "What's all this noise? All this foot-stomping?" The father said, "Son, your brother has just come home."

"So what? Is that why you killed the fatted calf? Is that why you ordered all this celebrating?"

"Yes, because he has come home, and the lost is found, and the dead has come back to life."

"That useless kid? That hippie? That beatnik? Running around with prostitutes? You never did anything like that for me. You never gave me a new coat or a gold ring. You never killed a calf for me! Oh, no, I can do my dancing with a scythe. You had me out there in the heat working my head off, and for that dude you pay out cash, and when he fouls up you give him a feast."

The father said, "Son, listen, it's all yours. Everything I have belongs to you. Come on, join the party."

"No. Oh no. No, this is not right. It's not just."

Salvation was never intended to be just. We're not saved by justice. As the dying Irishman said when they told him he was going to a just reward, "Justice! . . . that's the one thing I don't want! I want mercy!"

Our God is a God of mercy.[7] And this boy who called in on the radio program was like the elder brother. He said, "There's a party going on and I'm out of it."

There are Christians today—substantial, office-bearing Christians—who have become elder brothers. I heard about one deacon, 60 years old, who, they said, had been a deacon for 40 years and was just as mean now as the day he was ordained. He didn't realize that, as Francis Schaeffer said, "God means Christianity to be fun."[8] Is that what you're missing? God's crepe suzettes? I wonder sometimes whether the whole church, instead of being the bride of Christ, has actually become the elder brother and a party pooper, while the rest of humanity out there in the athletic stadium seems to fit as the prodigal in the parable.

People tell me that Christianity is about suffering, not joy, because Jesus suffered and died on the cross. But what was it that made Him suffer? What made Him a man of sorrows? *Our sins* made Him suffer. We put a crown of thorns on Him and whipped Him, and we punished Him on the cross for something He didn't do.

But Jesus did not stay in the tomb. He came out of the tomb on Easter morning. And that first word He spoke on Easter morning to Mary (Matthew 28:9) as He came out of the tomb—do you remember it? It was *chairete*, meaning "Take joy!" Jesus was on His way to joy, and when He left in a cloud, His disciples didn't weep. They were filled with joy. Do you have resurrection joy? Would you like to delight yourself in the Lord? You can.

EIGHTEEN

The Secret of Radiance

Then, in such hour of need
Of our fainting, dispirited race,
You, like angels, appear
Radiant with ardor divine!

—MATTHEW ARNOLD IN RUGBY CHAPEL

RADIANCE TO ME IS NOT HEAT waves from a fireplace or a radiator. Rather it is a quality of joy, much in the way that joy was and is a quality of Jesus of Nazareth, the Son of God. Beginning His ministry at 30 years of age, this young man showed such radiance of spirit that the common people of His day found Him hard to resist. There was a buoyancy about Him, a freedom and openness—yes, and a gladness and merriment as He set about doing His Father's will. Men, women, and children all found Him appealing, sometimes in contrast to other religious types.

Jesus never seems to have traded on His personality. He coveted no honors and anticipated no glory except the role of a servant. Most of the time He was unwilling to talk about Himself. Instead He would ask, "Who do people say that I am?" We look in vain for expressions from Him such as "my power," "my wisdom," "my significance," "my reverence" or "my holiness."

He did mention one characteristic of Himself worth examining. In John 15 and 17 He spoke of "my joy." It was not an honor He earned or developed; it was just part of Him that He brought from heaven. While He was addressing His Father in the great prayer of John 17, Jesus said, "I am coming to you now, but I say these things while I am still in the world, so that they may have the full measure of my joy within them."[1]

"My joy." If you wonder what gave Jesus' face such a radiance that He instinctively drew all kinds of men, women and children to Himself, you may find a clue here. His joy was not an attribute or a characteristic of Him so much as it was a kind of radiating of Himself. So why did He single out joy for emphasis? I can think of no reason for speaking of "my joy" beyond the fact that He must have been in Himself a radiant, Spirit-filled Person.

Henry Alford, Dean of Canterbury and a compiler of the Greek New Testament, believes that when Jesus spoke of "my joy" He was referring not to His camaraderie with His disciples or His enjoyment of the Palestinian environment. Rather He was reflecting "His holy exultation in the love of His Father."[2] His joy was the "joy of the Lord" that the prophet Nehemiah in the Old Testament declared "is your strength." It comes to us as an inner joy that radiates from God and remains untouchable even in the worst of times. It kept Jesus radiating good cheer wherever He happened to be, even in a sinking boat.

This quality, "my joy," was what Jesus came to bring *us* as an accompaniment to our salvation. He said explicitly in John 15, "These things I have spoken to you that My joy may remain in you, and that your joy may be full." Once His joy is implanted in us, He said, He wants it to become our joy, our unique and permanent possession. It then becomes something that can no more be taken from us than Jesus' own joy could be taken from Him. He wants joy to radiate from us as it did from Him, and He wants our joy to be *full*. He wants it to be jubilant, exultant, merry, brimful, and spilling over. Not obnoxious, of course; not oh-so-jolly, or put on as a professional clown puts on his painted smile and costume, but real, sturdy, and contagious, a light touch able to bolster people's spirits in the midst of tough situations.

Arthur John Gossip tells us that in the book of Acts the disciples caught the joy of Jesus, that "always their eyes are shining, always their hearts dance and exult in the sheer delight of what they have found—the splendor and the joy of it. They coin new words. They invent superlatives. But in the end they frankly confess they have given no idea of it."[3]

I want a radiance like that. I join with Oswald Chambers in saying, "May the Lord keep me radiantly and joyously His." Those who know me might wonder why instead of asking God for "radiance" I don't ask Him to do something about my own obvious personality defects. Sorry, but it's too late. There's not much He can do about my personality warts. That doesn't mean I can't make the effort to be a more amiable person, and all that. But to get to heaven I am depending solely on the blood of Jesus and the amazing grace of God, who loves me and understands my predicament.

Would you like a radiant glow? Would you like the iridescent glory of the Holy Spirit to be visible on your face so that it might reflect on those you may encounter? That's a large order, and it might do well for us to take a good look at what the Bible means by the word "radiant."

The word is found often in the NIV translation. In Exodus 34:29 we read, "When Moses came down from Mount Sinai with the tablets of the Testimony in his hands, he was not aware that his face was radiant because he had spoken with the LORD." *The Living Bible* also uses the word "radiate" to describe the face of the Lord God Himself. A famous benediction that God gave to Moses and Aaron contains the words "May the Lord bless and protect you; may the Lord's face radiate with joy because of you; may he be gracious to you, show you his favor, and give you his peace" (Numbers 6:24-26).

The New Testament translations of the Gospel of Matthew all say that when Jesus ascended the Mount of Transfiguration,

His face "shone like the sun." Dean Alford suggests that Jesus' face was "lighted with radiance both from without and within."[4] Was He smiling? The record does not say.

In the Random House dictionary the word "radiance" is listed as having two meanings. One has to do with light and its warm, shining effect. The second has to do with such subjects as joy and hope, as in "a radiant smile" and "a radiant future."

At the birth of Jesus the light of heaven created a radiance that seems always to have surrounded the Christmas season since the early centuries. The stars shone down on shepherds in the fields outside Bethlethem as they tended their flocks, and the angels brought glad tidings of great joy and peace. Later the light from a particular star guided the magi or "wise men from the East" who crossed the desert to find the dwelling place of the Christ child.

It is worth asking why Christmas (despite some modern attempts to eliminate it from American culture) is universally the most popular holiday in the calendar. Due in large part to the labors of missionaries past and present, it is celebrated today more than ever, not only in Western countries but also around the world.

I'll tell you what makes Christmas popular: It is the radiance that comes from the face of Jesus Christ. Year after year Jesus continues to shed a radiant glow over the Christmas season. He is the watershed between life's goodness and badness. We express that truth by singing songs and hymns, by sending greeting cards and exchanging presents, by attending special church services and family gatherings. The joy of Christmas is very real, even though many people manage to miss it.

Some fascinating uses of the word "radiance" are found in the Old Testament. Shulamith, in the Song of Songs, describes her lover as "radiant and ruddy." Psalm 19 speaks of the commands of the Lord as "radiant." And Ezekiel in his great vision sees the land of Israel itself as "radiant with His glory."

Just glance at a few of the words commonly associated with this one word "radiant": ebullient, ecstatic, elated, glad, enraptured, euphoric, exuberant, exultant, jocund, jubilant, mirthful, merry, animate, hilarious. You'll find them all in the English Bible in one translation or another.

In a rare moment during His ministry Jesus declared, "I am the light of the world. He who follows Me shall not walk in darkness, but have the light of life" (John 8:12). A confirmation of that assertion is found in the letter to the Hebrews: "The Son is the radiance of God's glory and the exact representation of his being" (1:3 NIV). One clear message of the whole New Testament is that *the radiance of Jesus has come down and is available to us!* The apostle Paul wrote to the church in Ephesus that Christ Himself anticipated a "radiant church."

It has been my privilege to worship God in churches on six continents: Brethren assemblies in New Zealand; a GI Quonset hut in the Aleutian Islands; white-painted meetinghouses in New England; a cardboard church in an Oregon city where whiskey glasses were used to serve communion; gigantic Roman, Anglican, and Russian Orthodox cathedrals in Europe; missionary churches in Samoa and the Yukon; Presbyterian churches in Brazil, Korea, and South Africa; indigenous churches in Jamaica and St. Lawrence island; a skyscraper in Hong Kong.

Did I find radiance in these churches? Yes! But let me tell you about a man in a particular church in southern California. This church is known the world over as Calvary Chapel. Located in lower Costa Mesa in what was once called the "Gospel Swamp," the church had a membership of 25 in 1970 when it called as its pastor a onetime Foursquare Gospel preacher named Charles Ward Smith. Today 35,000 people pass through its buildings every week.

Mr. Smith, known over the world as "Chuck," had dropped out of the ministry in his younger days, discouraged, and had turned to cleaning carpets and building houses. On the side he taught the Bible in home groups. But soon he resumed his ministry in Calvary Chapel, and a spiritual explosion took place among West Coast young people who became known as the "Jesus Generation."

Who were these young people? Actually a lot of them were "flower children," druggies who had been frightened out of their skins by demons appearing in their dreams. Trips "way out" on LSD, cocaine, and methamphetamine drugs had produced nightmares of sheer terror. Many of them came from good homes. They cried out, calling on the one Name they remembered from childhood who had authority over the demons: *Jesus.* It worked.

Grateful for deliverance, hundreds and thousands of them began swarming into Pacific Coast churches during the late 60s and 70s. Unwashed, longhaired, barefoot, wearing earrings and unkempt clothing, they dropped their joints outside on the church sidewalk, flushed their hard drugs down the church toilets, and slumped into the church pews, where they tried sticking their bare toes through the communion cup holders.

Chuck Smith and his wife Kay went out of their way to befriend the young people. The word spread quickly among the communes: Calvary Chapel, Costa Mesa had a welcome mat. It soon became an unoffical gathering place for the movement.

Today Chuck Smith has passed his seventieth birthday. His four children are grown. The fringe of hair around his handsome bald head has turned white. But his frame is still stocky, and his broad smile is as radiant as it was when the Jesus people responded to it by pouring into his church back in the 1970s. One such, responding at age 26, was the man who later became my pastor, Dr. Michael MacIntosh, founding minister of Horizon Christian Fellowship, San Diego.

What is it about Chuck Smith?[5] People say that it is the joy and peace on his countenance. It is a benign, genuine expression of goodness, righteousness, and love. However you describe it, it makes people feel good just to look at him. What about his Bible-believing theology, his position on sin and trust in the supernatural? Yes, that is all part of Chuck. What about his love for Jesus? *Yes!* That is the real source of his radiance.

NINETEEN

Joy and Overjoy

*You may have the joy-bells
ringing in your heart.*

—J. EDWIN RUARK

∿

THE JOY OF THE LORD is sometimes described as a quiet, warm, loving sense of intimate relationship with the Creator through His Son, Jesus Christ. It is not necessarily a tiptoe experience, full of ecstasy or ebullience; nor does it flicker on and off like a tired light bulb. It does not depend upon emotional experiences ("I just found my glasses!" or "I just won the lottery!"). The joy that comes from Jesus by the Holy Spirit is always bound up with the written Word of God, where inspiration keeps love flowing through the pipeline.

Given the fact that the joy of heaven is a steady radiant light, there are still rare times in the life of God's people when the Almighty chooses to send a dazzling shaft of glory into the life of a believer. One of the newer Bible translations from the Greek renders the word *agalliasis* with the word "overjoy." I know many Christians who can testify to the reality of an overjoy experience in their lives.

Lori Connett is one. She writes me, "The most elated moment of joy that I can ever recall is when my husband, Ed, accepted the Lord as his Savior. That day my joy was truly made full and I rejoiced with the angels."

Eric Thompson is another. He writes me, "I have experienced joy that feels like a well of water springing up inside me when I am thanking God for saving me from a very deep and terrible pit. In that moment I truly know who I am and who God is."

Life for Christians is not always easy, and many wonderful group Bible studies are available these days, seeking to help people to resolve some of the difficulties and challenges that they have to face in life. I have been helped by such studies, and I thank God for them. It is because our book has a rather uncommon purpose that in this chapter we shall strike a different note. We're going for the joy. We shall see what the Bible says about believers who have found themselves in a glowing, lifting, enraptured state of "overjoyment!"

GOD'S MIRACULOUS PROTECTION

Our first story is one of the all-time favorites in the Bible.[1] It tells of a king named Darius the Mede, who ruled a country named Babylon (now Iraq) which had just been conquered by his army of Medes and Persians. One of the conquered citizens of Babylon was a Hebrew prophet named Daniel or Belteshazzar. He had held a high position in the Babylonian government and was now equally well regarded by the new King Darius, who considered him a fine statesman.

Daniel had enemies, however, and they informed King Darius that Daniel had violated the king's own recent religious edict by praying to the God of the Hebrews. Darius personally made an effort to save the man, but was unsuccessful in having his own royal law annulled, which called for the violator to be thrown to the lions.

As he issued the decree, King Darius expressed the hope to Daniel that his God would rescue him. That evening the king was disturbed, and canceled his usual entertainment (the Hebrew word here, according to Delitzsch, is "concubines") and went to bed but could not sleep. At daybreak King Darius hurried to the lions' den, ordered the royal seal broken and the stone rolled back, then called out, "Daniel, servant of the living God, has your God . . . been able to deliver you from the lions?"

The Scripture record indicates that Daniel gave a joyful shout, "O king, live forever! My God sent His angel and shut the lions' mouths, so that they have not hurt me."[2] He might have added (as I heard a black preacher relate this story), "Ever since you sealed me in here, O King, those big cats have been purring up a storm and rubbing themselves against my legs!"

Daniel 6:23 NIV says that King Darius himself "was overjoyed" at the intervention of Daniel's God. He proceeded, pagan fashion, to throw Daniel's enemies into the den, where their reception was not so friendly. The record states further that Daniel "prospered" during King Darius' reign, and that the king issued yet another decree praising the "living God" of Daniel.[3]

GOD'S DIVINE GUIDANCE

Our next story is about the first of many millions of non-Jewish or Gentile seekers to come to Jesus.[4] They came early, when Jesus was probably under two years of age. They were magi or astrologers, probably from the region around Iraq, who said they had seen a strange star in the heavens and had interpreted it as signifying the birth of the "king of the Jews."

These "wise men" (we don't know how many there were) undoubtedly came across the desert by caravan, intending to worship the child and to offer gifts. They went to King Herod's palace in Jerusalem and inquired of him where the royal child was. Herod in turn inquired of the temple rabbis and learned that the prophet Micah had predicted the birth of such a ruler in nearby Bethlehem.[5]

Herod sensed in the arrival of the magi a threat to his own throne, and asked the visitors to notify him after they had located the child so that he too might "worship Him." The men went on and discovered that the star they had seen in the East had reappeared and was now going before them. It led them until it "stood over where the young child was." The King James record then says, "When they saw the star, they rejoiced with exceedingly great joy."[6] The magi then entered the house, greeted Mary, worshiped the infant Jesus, and presented gifts. After days and weeks of difficult travel, the magi had reached their goal and were overjoyed. Then, warned in a timely dream, they gave King Herod the slip and returned home by a different route.

THE LORD APPEARS TO HIS OWN

Next we come to a dramatic late-night meeting of some of the disciples in a locked room in Jerusalem. The strange things that occurred in that room are described in Mark 16, Luke 24, and John 20. At first the men were utterly grief-stricken and weeping as the loss of their Leader was borne in upon them. Then someone came in and reported that Peter had seen Jesus alive after the crucifixion![7]

This news seemed so preposterous that no one believed it. But soon afterward Cleopas and his companion came in, breathless from their night travel, and said Jesus had walked with them on the road to Emmaus and had shared a meal with them. This too seemed incredible.

In 1 Corinthians 15:7 the apostle Paul states that after His resurrection Jesus appeared to His half-brother James, as well as to others. Those incidents probably occurred later, but it is worth speculating whether James might also have come into the room that night with word that he had seen Jesus. Someone else might have reported that some women had seen Jesus near the tomb.

Just imagine the excitement and pandemonium that must have prevailed in that room! They were already terrified by the religious opposition and had to keep the door bolted. Three days after His death on the cross and His burial in the tomb, here were people saying they had seen Jesus alive. Were they seeing ghosts? What was going on? Some continued to weep, but others began to wonder and even tremble. Was God doing something? Was this another miracle? Or was it the end of everything?

Then suddenly Jesus Himself appeared. Great fear swept through the room, mixed with wonder, doubt, disbelief, and then, amazingly, joy. Jesus smiled, gave a greeting of peace, visited with His disciples, showed them His hands, His feet, and His side, and asked for something to eat. They gave Him a piece of broiled fish and a honeycomb, and He ate.[8]

It took awhile for the disciples to believe that the last enemy, death, had really lost its sting and the grave had really been defeated. At last they came to recognize Him and were fully conscious that the Man standing alive in their midst and talking with them was the Master whom they had just seen crucified. The text in John says it well: "The disciples were overjoyed when they saw the Lord."[9]

GOD HEARS HIS CHURCH'S PRAYER

For our fourth story we begin with Peter's miraculous escape from prison in Jerusalem and his visit to a group of believers who had been praying for him.[10] Peter's arrest came during a persecution instigated by the tetrarch Herod Antipas, son of Herod the Great, during the Days of Unleavened Bread. When Herod saw that the Jerusalem rabble applauded his execution of the apostle James (brother of John), he had Peter arrested and confined overnight, planning to execute him the next day.

While prayers were being offered to God for Peter by the young church, four quaternions of soldiers were assigned to guard Peter overnight in the prison. The 16 men were divided Roman style into four watches of three hours each. Peter slept chained to a soldier on either side while the other two guards kept watch at the door. Herod's plan was to keep Peter in custody until after the Passover observance, then to present him before the people for the death sentencing.

During the fourth watch of the night, between 3 and 6 A.M., an angel appeared and struck the chains off Peter's wrists, then told him to put on his clothes, sandals, and cloak and "follow me." Peter rose, and incredibly they passed the first guard station, then another, and finally came to a large locked iron door that led to the street. It seems the door opened "of its own accord," and they passed through and descended the steps, after which the angel disappeared. Only then did Peter grasp that what he thought was a dream was a miracle, and he was a free man.

Walking quickly, Peter arrived at a "safe house" where lived Mary, the mother of John Mark and aunt of Barnabas. Here occurred one of those little incidents that reveal the way people really act in abnormal situations. It helps to confirm us in the belief that the Bible is a faithful record.

Peter knocked at the door of the gate, and a young girl named Rhoda came to answer. She was one of a group of Christians who had been meeting in the house all night apparently, praying for Peter's deliverance from what seemed certain death. Whether it was still dark is not clear, but when Rhoda opened the door she recognized Peter's voice and was filled with joy. So overjoyed was she that instead of opening the gate so he could come in, she turned and ran back inside to announce to the prayer group that Peter was out there standing at the gate.

The other Christians inside refused to believe her, and when Rhoda insisted, they decided it must be "Peter's angel." Meanwhile Peter himself was left outside knocking until finally the door and the gate were opened and he walked in, to everyone's astonishment. As with Rhoda, the joy of the believers must have known no bounds as they looked at the living answer to their prayers.

Peter didn't stay long, but he did take time to tell his friends about the angel and the prison escape. Presumably he partook of some refreshment; and before leaving he asked that they "tell these things to James [the Lord's brother] and to the brethren." He then left, and later in the book of Acts Peter is seen participating in the first church council in Jerusalem.[11] As for the hapless prison guards in the fourth watch, they were executed by royal order.[12]

MY CUP RUNNETH OVER

The word "overjoyed" is an English translation of the Greek word *agalliasis*, which is also rendered "exultation" and "exuberant joy." It appears in many significant places in the Bible in addition to those just described.

Luke uses the word twice in the first chapter of his Gospel, 1:14 and 1:44. The priest Zacharias was informed that his wife, Elizabeth, would bear a son (John the Baptist), and that "you will have joy and gladness" and that "many will rejoice at his birth." Later his wife, Elizabeth, received a visit from her cousin Mary, and the Holy Spirit informed her that Mary would give birth to the Messiah. Elizabeth addressed Mary as "the mother of my Lord" (1:43) and told Mary that when she first heard Mary's greeting, her own unborn baby *leaped in my womb for joy.*"

In Acts 2:46,47 Luke gives a warmhearted description of the early church as he writes: "Continuing daily with one accord in the temple, and breaking bread from house to house, they ate their food with gladness and simplicity of heart, praising God and having favor with all the people. And the Lord added to the church daily those who were being saved."

In the letter to the Hebrews the author addresses Jesus in these words taken from Psalm 45:7: "You love righteousness and hate wickedness; therefore God, Your God, has anointed You with the *oil of gladness* more than Your companions." That verse seems to tell us convincingly that in the opinion of those who knew Him and loved Him, Jesus was a man of joy.

The word "overjoyed" (*agalliasis*) appears finally in the closing verses of the letter of Jude (24,25). I first heard that magnificent benediction when I was eight years old: "Now unto him who is able to keep you from falling, and to present you faultless before the presence of his glory *with exceeding joy*, to the only wise God our Savior, be glory and majesty, dominion and power, both now and ever. Amen."

Those words from the King James Bible were first recited to me and my brother in 1919 by my father's diminutive, devout, withering elder sister, Julia J. MacPherson, as she stood before us in her little cottage in Saranap, California.[13]

Aunt Julia had no children. Her husband had left her and disappeared. She spent her retirement years writing poems for the *Walnut Creek Weekly*, and sharing with her poor neighbors her Western Union pension and the cherries from her tiny orchard. She died in 1946 at age 99 years 11 months, and is now in heaven, filled, I trust, with *agalliasis*!

Since joy and laughter have played such vital roles in the lives of Christians for two thousand years, why don't you use the rest of this page to write an experience of your own of being overjoyed by the presence of God in your life?

Glorious Promise

TWENTY

Faith Creating Joy

A little faith will bring your soul to heaven,
but a lot of faith will bring
heaven to your soul.

—DWIGHT L. MOODY

FAITH. WHAT A MAGNIFICENT WORD! In five letters it just about sums up the whole Christian life. Did you think when you picked up this book that in it you might find something about the joy of the Lord? You were right, but you will never find that joy without faith. You might be curious enough to ask, "What does he mean by that? Faith in what? What is faith?"

Put simply, Christian faith is believing that Jesus died for you and me. He died on the cross to take away our sins. He made His vicarious sacrifice at Calvary for us, on our behalf and in our stead, and He rose again the third day.

That is the indispensable start. If your answer to that statement is "I do believe," you have just made an act of faith. Then the inspired word of the apostle Paul applies to you. He wrote to the church in Rome, "If you confess with your mouth the Lord Jesus and believe in your heart that God has raised Him from the dead, you will be saved."[1]

If your response again is "I confess and believe," no one on earth or in heaven can successfully question your right to be called a believing Christian. Here is the apostle's confirming word: "By grace you have been saved through faith, and that not of yourselves; it is the gift of God, not of works, lest anyone should boast."[2]

What else do you need? Nothing . . . for salvation. Well, what else is there? There is more explaining of what those words mean that you have just accepted and embraced. And then there is joy, the joy of faith, the joy of loving Jesus, the anticipation of the delights of heaven.

What is faith? I like this word of explanation by an English theologian, W. A. Whitehouse: "Faith is the act by which a person lays hold on God's resources, becomes obedient to what God prescribes, and, abandoning all self-interest and self-reliance, trusts God completely."[3] In other words, we forget about ourselves and put ourselves in God's hands. We trust Him. We trust His goodness and His love. We trust His firmness, steadfastness, and total reliability. He is our Father, and we love Him.

The letter to the Hebrews says that "faith is the substance of things hoped for, the evidence of things not seen."[4] That definition, you can see, is generic rather than specific. It shows that faith has a spiritual reality of its own, just as valid in its own way as reason and knowledge. And the "faith" referred to is clearly faith in the Good News of Jesus Christ.

Hundreds of years before Christ, the prophet Habakkuk was the first to write these wonderful words: "The just shall live by his faith."[5] The apostle Paul used them later in his letter to the Romans to establish the Christian doctrine of justification by faith. It means that when we believe in Christ our sins are forgiven; Christ Himself has atoned for them. We can accept that fact, and we don't need to work out some penitential payment for them. We stand justified before God, with our sins vanished into oblivion.

The reformer Martin Luther made "justification by faith" the keystone of the Spirit-led Reformation of the sixteenth century, and he clarified it by adding the word "alone." We are justified by faith in Christ *alone*. We are saved by grace through faith *alone*.

For people who have no knowledge of it, faith sometimes seems a confusing thing. Many reject it. H.L. Mencken, an American journalist, once defined faith as "an illogical belief in the occurrence of the improbable." Ernest Hemingway, for a crude joke, once changed the Lord's Prayer to "our nada who art in nada, nada be thy nada." (*Nada* is the Spanish word for "nothing.")

And yet despite such scorners and cynics, faith is what keeps us alive. I wouldn't have stepped out of bed this morning if I hadn't had faith that the floor would hold me. Josh Billings carries it further: "If it weren't for faith, there would be no living in this world; we couldn't even eat hash!"[6] I wouldn't finish this sentence on the computer if I did not have faith that one day you would read it!

Faith is one of God's greatest gifts. In the Bible, one finds faith clearly illustrated in three incidents. The first is found in the Old Testament Book of Genesis, describing Abraham's sacrifice of his son Isaac.[7] At the command of God, Abraham prepared to offer his young son on a sacrificial altar. Abraham supernaturally demonstrated great faith in that act, and it leaves us awash in admiration. God recognized that He had a man prepared to do anything to prove his trust in his Lord. In Hebrews 11:19 we learn Abraham believed that even if he carried out the sacrificial act, God could raise up his son from the dead, because He had promised to create a great nation from his offspring. Abraham was saved from sacrificing Isaac by an angel and the presence of a ram caught in the brush. Thus Abraham became a man of honor, worthy to be called God's friend and to be the spiritual father of all believers.

The Bible also illustrates faith in a marvelous way in the entire eleventh chapter of the letter to the Hebrews. What an inspiring panorama of spiritual greatness! Here are paraded all the heroes of faith, men and women of Hebrew history known and unknown from Abraham down to David and the prophets "who through faith subdued kingdoms, worked righteousness, obtained promises, stopped the mouths of lions . . . of whom the world was not worthy."[8]

As a follower of Jesus, I can applaud and admire all these superb heroes of faith; and there are more. What of James the brother of John the apostle, and Stephen, Peter, Paul, and the many other heroes of the first century? Once I published a book titled *Faith's Heroes* which honored men and women of succeeding centuries who exercised great faith in their ministry. Among them were Polycarp, Vibia Perpetua, Augustine, Francis of Assisi, Martin Luther, Ulrich Zwingli, George Fox, George Whitefield, Amy Carmichael, and others.

But now the record must be set straight.

What Abraham had I do not seem to have. It is not a question of sacrifice; I would gladly sacrifice myself for members of my family and for others, too, as circumstances required. But when it comes to sacrificing someone else—I pass. This is a test of faith. Augustine's friend Alypius read Paul's letter to the Romans and then declared that since God would apparently accept someone with weak faith (Romans 14:1), he would become a Christian. I think I side with Bishop Alypius, not with Abraham.

In the same way, I find myself unqualified when I examine the list of men and women of faith as we find it in the eleventh chapter of Hebrews. They demonstrated a magnificent faith in God, a supreme gift of the Holy Spirit. I admire them and would love to emulate them, but as with Alypius, my faith is weak and I feel unworthy.

The third place where we find great faith is in the words of Jesus, as found in Matthew 17:20: "I say to you, if you have faith as a mustard seed, you will say to this mountain, 'Move from here to there,' and it will move; and nothing will be impossible for you."

Now there is a challenge from the Lord Jesus Christ Himself that takes one's breath away. Move a mountain by sheer faith? A whole mountain, like Kilimanjaro? What could Jesus have been thinking of? It makes no sense whatever.

Or does it? Yes, it does. Excuse me, but by the grace of God I gladly fall in line when those saints go marching in. Move a whole massive mountain by faith? Absolutely. I have done it—by faith. I have watched amazed as a whole mountain of grief and anger rolled right off my back and never returned. I have also seen other hard-pressed Christians kneel and go to the cross with Jesus in tears, and then stand up and shake off one mountain after another that had been squatting on them and crushing their weary spirits.

How did it all happen? Not by any human agency, unless you want to credit a microscopic grain of faith. It was actually done by the power and favor and love of the Holy Spirit in answer to that tiny bit of faith. It fills me with hilarity (a good Bible word) to think of it. Confession? Yes. Repentance? Absolutely. Faith, prayer, intercession? Of course. But no transcripts. No track record. No diplomas, resumes, degrees, honors, letters of commendation, holy garments, or press clippings. Just Jesus.

How about you? Have you been that route? Let me make a suggestion. Go out to the nearest garden and pick up a seed the size of a tiny mustard seed. Let that be the size of your faith. Now use it.

There remains the question, Where is the joy in all this? When faith is put to work, where does the joy come in? The answer of the Bible is that *the faith itself creates the joy.* Faith leads to contentment, and contentment leads to peace, and peace brings into play all the other fruits of the Spirit, including love and joy.

Faith goes with the Christian wherever he or she goes. It is not easy to describe the electric spark, the inner thrill that comes to a believer when he meets someone else who is "of the faith." The welcoming smile, the murmuring of the name of Jesus—any one of a hundred looks and gestures can bring recognition and response, and the beginning of a friendship that has its basis in the heaven of heavens. Jesus said, "Where two or three are gathered together in My name, there am I in the midst of them,"[9] and it is still true. Thus does my Jesus share the faith, and the faith creates the joy.

Older believers meet and encourage each other. They reminisce, calling up memories of great spiritual events of faith. Middle-aged people revel in the signs of growing faith in their children. Young people find tremendous support in their own walk with Jesus as they fellowship with like-minded young believers. The joy of the Lord adds strength to their spiritual commitment.

All of this sharing of the faith brings gladness of heart to believers who may well be undergoing life's trials. What a blessing it is to meet a lighthearted Christian who believes what Jesus says: that His yoke is easy and His burden is light.[10] There is such a joy in the faith itself, in the knowledge that our lives are in God's hands and that eventually everything will "pan out" all right.

Many books have been written about faith, and with good reason, for faith has always meant different things to different people. The very word "faith" to many people conjures up windmills in the head and an imaginary environment. For such doubters faith is equivalent to a lie, for it seems to accept as fact what they are sure "isn't so." I know, because for years faith meant little or nothing to me.

By contrast, for millions of God's people faith has always been a lifeboat in a stormy sea. It equips the believer with wisdom and confidence in discerning the doubter's error and the cynic's lie. No one slickers his way into the kingdom of heaven! When doubts and false reasoning and disastrous outward circumstances combine to confuse the believer, faith provides an armor of protection. It leads the believer along a path of righteousness which is patrolled by angels and protected by God Himself.

Faith has a way of bringing about the joy of spiritual freedom. We are relieved to know that God is not looking over our "good works," which are always subject to the flaws of personal ego. God is rather looking at our faith in Him. We don't have to earn our way to Him because He is already with us. When trouble comes, He assures us that it will not last. "Fret not."[11] When our hopes for income are disappointed, Jesus sends us His message: "Do not worry."[12] The French have a saying, "ça passe." Whatever it is, it will go away in time. Good things lie ahead. Take joy.

Perhaps the greatest joy of all for the Christian is to lead someone else into the presence of God and then see the Holy Spirit bring that person to Himself. Nothing in the world can make God so real to us—or so awesome—as to realize that He is using us (sinners that we are) to win another person to Jesus Christ. One of the nobler things Billy Graham has done for the church has been to offer a simple prayer for a person seeking Christ. I have heard him say it many times, and I have used it with members of my own family:

"Oh God, I am a sinner. I am sorry for my sins. I am willing to turn from my sins. I receive Jesus Christ as my Savior. I confess Him as my Lord. From this moment I want to follow Him and serve Him in the fellowship of His church."

Jesus said that there is great joy in heaven among the angels when a sinner repents.[13] It may be in a great meeting, or it may be a very unimposing scene in a small church, or in a living room or dormitory with few people present. When those words are repeated—or words like them—by a sincere seeker in faith, you can be sure that the Holy Spirit is at work, and that at the portals of glory there is celebrating among the angels.

Where is the joy in saving faith? It is the joy of Jesus, that which He called "my joy." To get you to that joy, perhaps this analogy will help.

When my brother Lincoln and I went camping as Boy Scouts we would sit around the campfire at night along with the other boys, warming ourselves and singing songs, after which our scoutmaster would regale us with scary stories right out of Arthur Conan Doyle. The night wind was chilly, but my brother and I were having fun because we shared a secret.

Under the embers of that bonfire we had hidden some Idaho potatoes (don't ask where we got them), and all evening long we had the joy of this assurance: that the spuds were there in the fire and that they were being roasted. When the blaze was being extinguished as time neared for "lights out," we reached in with sticks and uncovered our treasure. Peeling off the black skin, we sank our teeth into the hot baked potatoes, and oh! did they taste good!

Would you like to make a test of secret faith? Make a spiritual investment outside your family, in a child, in a church, in some kind of spiritual mission or goal. This is your hidden "hot potato," your secret with Jesus. After awhile rake it out of the fire, peel off the black skin, and bite it.

Sink your teeth into your secret investment. Taste it. Enjoy it. See how good God is, and what your faith has done for you!

TWENTY-ONE

Hope That Brings Joy

The opposite of joy is not sorrow.
It is unbelief.

—LESLIE WEATHERHEAD

⌇

THE LEAST JOYOUS PASSAGE in the Bible is not found among the Old Testament threats of judgment or in the weeping prophets. The least joyous passage is in Paul's first letter to the Corinthians. In it he writes, "If Christ has not been raised, your faith is futile; you are still in your sins." Paul expands: "If only for this life we have hope in Christ, we are to be pitied more than all men."[1]

For two thousand years the cross has been the symbol of Christianity. We see it everywhere—on churches, on necklaces, on the front of Bibles, in cemeteries, on mountaintops. It bears silent witness to our salvation through the atonement of Jesus Christ, whose vicarious sacrifice for our sins paved for us the highway to heaven, taking us from death to life eternal. To Christians of every persuasion it is more precious than life. We love it. But there is another symbol of Christianity that has a different but vital place in the hearts of us who believe, and that is the empty tomb.

It has been said often over the past two thousand years that the Christian church was built on the resurrection of Jesus Christ from that tomb. The apostle Paul opens his letter to the Romans with the statement that Jesus Christ our Lord was "declared to be the Son of God with power, according to the Spirit of holiness, *by the resurrection from the dead.*"[2]

John Whale was right when he wrote, "The church of Christ owes its very existence to the fact that in this open graveyard of the world there is one gaping tomb, one rent sepulchre. Belief in the resurrection is not an appendage to the Christian faith; it *is* the Christian faith. The Gospels cannot explain the resurrection, it is the resurrection alone which explains the Gospels."[3]

Let's go over it again very simply. A Man was born, lived, and grew to maturity. He was put to death by execution and was buried in a grave. Three days later His grave was found empty. It was thought His body had been stolen. Then He was sighted. Hundreds of people saw Him. Some heard Him speak, others watched Him eat, still others examined the wounds that killed Him. Then, after some meetings with His followers, He disappeared. His bones were never found.

The resurrection story was not built on human credulity or inventiveness. The man involved was not Elvis Presley, nor was He Harry Houdini. The man was Jesus of Nazareth, the Son of God, who was said to be "risen indeed" and who "has become the firstfruits of those who have fallen asleep." Paul wrote to the Philippians that "God has highly exalted" His Son, and he wrote to the Colossians that Jesus Christ was also "head of the . . . church" and that "in Him all things consist . . . that . . . He may have the preeminence."[4]

But the overwhelming effect of this alive-from-the-dead report was not just on the people involved in what happened— the temple guards, the Sanhedrin, the disciples, the women, and the others who may have talked with the risen Jesus. The most amazing thing was what the resurrection did to you and me! It gave us hope beyond death.

Here is a three-year-old boy whose father was just killed in a skiing accident. His little world is destroyed. His Christian mother comforts him: "Dear, Jesus came back from the grave and told us that one day we will see Daddy again. When we get to heaven he'll be waiting for us." The boy believes her. Our visions of heaven may be misty, it's true, but there was nothing cloudy about the resurrection: It actually happened. There are days for all of us when the thought of Jesus' empty tomb can fill our hearts with hope and joy.

The Bible claims that with Jesus' resurrection the fortifications of the last enemy, death, were breached. So if Jesus made it through the cycle of birth and death and came out alive, what about us? Since the beginning of life on earth the different cultures have all had their immortality legends about some Elysium or Happy Hunting Ground. Learning about such legends is a part of growing up. We don't of course believe them. We find them interesting and let the anthropologists write books about them, but they remain legends.

Now we are faced with a document that claims authenticity, not about a "beautiful isle of somewhere," but about an actual occurrence at a point in time, when someone who was dead came back to life. So if it happened to Him, what does it imply? Are we doomed to become fertilizer, or is there something more? Right now I am not especially concerned about what life after death will be like. If I can be with Jesus, that's all I could ask. Our Lord told His disciples, "I will come again and receive you to Myself." I'm counting on that.

There is another side to joy, and that is *no* joy. Our runaway culture has forgotten that the Bible warns of coming judgment, both for human beings and for nations. People who ignore the teachings of the Bible and commit what the Bible calls "the works of the flesh" will be called to account. The choices of time are binding in eternity.

The whole prospect of the future is mysterious and beyond imagination, but because of the resurrection account I have hope, not just for me, but for all those who love Jesus. For those who fill our media with lust, crimes, wickedness, corruption, and horror, and for those who are wasting their lives in self-seeking, useless, soul-corrupting activities that the Bible calls sin, I will simply refer to Hebrews 10:31: "It is a fearful thing to fall into the hands of the living God." In a book on joy it is not congenial to discuss the temperature of hell, but it is nevertheless there waiting.

Here is a curious thing: Nearly all the books on aging today are written by younger experts. They cover everything connected with the subject of impending death. They consider the gradual disrepair of the body, the final medical report, the disposal of the remains, the funeral arrangements, the gravesite, the press notices, the will, the probate, the insurance, the division of the property, the settling of the accounts, the invitations to the memorial service, the seating of the immediate family, the inscription (if any) on the headstone, the quarreling among the heirs.

But God? Heaven? Judgment? "Good heavens! Who knows?"

Americans generally consider life itself to be a boon, and seek to protract it as long as possible. They may and do complain, but seem in no hurry to leave their present existence. Soldiers who returned from the Gulf War told how precious this life seemed to them, how wonderful it was just to be living at home.

We Christians are taught that life is a love gift from God and is to be lived in a spirit of thanksgiving; but the Bible also indicates that our time here on earth is a time of testing and preparation for a future life. These few years of ours on the planet are a dry run, a road test, a proving ground, a shakedown cruise, and a simulator flight. We are pilgrims passing through, joyous with hope.

You might say this world is a doughnut shop where we stop in for a cup of coffee and a raised doughnut before moving on. We are not headed for Basin Street or Las Vegas or Piccadilly Circus or the Champs d'Elysées or the Yellow Brick Road to the Emerald City of Oz. Our road map is the last two chapters of the book of Revelation. We are assured that what God has in mind for His children is so marvelous that it will make the whole global Internet system with its websites and cyberspace look like a child scrawling on a slate with a piece of chalk.

The late Carl Sagan assured us all that there is "nothing beyond the cosmos." I believe he has since then had some second thoughts about his statement. For us it is enough that Christ died for our sins according to the Scriptures, and was buried, and rose again the third day according to the Scriptures.

Today it is the continuing conviction of millions of Christians that Jesus' reappearance in the flesh following His crucifixion meant that there had been a resurrection from the dead. The natural processes of birth, life, and death were broken into, and the interruption was the deliberate, conscious act of the Supreme Creator of the universe. He who fixed the natural laws suspended them in this instance for a supernatural law. The famous objection of Professor Gotthold Lessing, a noted eighteenth-century German scholar, that "particular facts of history cannot establish eternal truths," was overridden on Easter morning by God Himself. The resurrection thereupon became an eternal truth.

But the glory of the resurrection did not end with the ascension of our Lord, as Luke tells us in the first chapter of the Acts of the Apostles. Such time as the risen Lord spent with us was a prelude to something that we Christians firmly believe is God's future purpose for His people. It is the "blessed hope," the return of the Lord Jesus Christ, His reentry into the earth's atmosphere as promised by the two men in white apparel on the Mount of Olives.

The scene is unforgettable. The disciples had just been talking with Jesus, and now He was gone, and the two men were standing there and saying, "Men of Galilee, why do you stand gazing up into heaven? This same Jesus, who was taken up from you into heaven, will so come in like manner as you saw Him go into heaven."[5] In other words, people, don't look back, look ahead!

All the history of the human race since that moment, all the explorations and wars and massacres and inventions and writings, all the good and evil statements and actions of men and women, all the progress and regress of the human race, are simply events bracketed in the time zone between the departure of our Lord and His soon return. And that's where we are at this moment.

Will tomorrow be a better day? In the twenty-first century will there be less cruelty and more love, less suffering and more joy? Is there a bright future on the horizon? Don't look to sociology or anthropology for the answer. They are in the bracket too. Look to Jesus. He is our hope.

Luke says that after our Lord blessed His disciples they then returned to Jerusalem "with great joy." They had the promise of the Spirit's power inscribed in their hearts. They had the love of God, the greatest thing in the universe, and it was their task to spread it to people everywhere until He comes. But the watchword is still "Lord, come quickly!"

When He comes, we who love Him shall go to meet Him. Then at last we shall know in all its pristine, unsullied fullness the *joy of the Lord*.

TWENTY-TWO

What's Amazing About Grace

*The surest mark of a Christian is not faith,
or even love, but joy.*

—SAMUEL M. SHOEMAKER

∽

AT THIS POINT IT IS POSSIBLE that we have enough evidence to say that Jesus came to earth on a joyous mission of salvation, and that one of His aims was that others might share that joy. Many people I have talked with acknowledge Jesus as the Author and Finisher of their faith, but they are wondering whether they might not have been missing something in their Christian lives. If Jesus had a secret, they don't know what it is. As for the New Testament's strong emphasis upon joy, they admit it didn't come through to them; they thought it was just preacher talk.

The time has come to say bluntly regarding this joy, "It sounds great if it's true," and then ask, "Where do we get it?"

To find out, we need to look at Jesus' mission. He came with orders to bring redemption to the human race, to draw men and women back to God, and to usher in His kingdom. After His baptism in the Jordan River He came into Galilee from the desert joyously, fresh from His victory over Satan, filled with the power of the Holy Spirit, and He launched His ministry on a high note. "The time has come," He announced. "The kingdom of God is near. Repent and believe the Good News."

This was uttered by no stern-faced prophet of doom. This was an elated, triumphant young Man saying, "Come! Join me! I know the way out of this. There is a good life, a great life. Take it from Me. Everything is ready. Come!"

And they did come, by the hundreds and the thousands. But even as we note the euphoria that accompanied this magnificent ministry, we should not lose sight of the fact that Jesus came to earth at His Father's behest and accomplished His earthly mission only with the supreme sacrifice of His own life. By dying upon the cross at Calvary and bearing our sins in His own body, Jesus removed the barrier between us and our Maker, and opened the gates of heaven to all who believe in Him.

The shedding of His blood upon the cross was not precipitated by mere action on the part of others. Jesus made it abundantly clear that His sacrifice was not intended to appease an angry deity; rather it was His own personal decision to carry out the work His beloved Father had commissioned Him to do.[1] "God was in Christ reconciling the world to Himself."[2] As the great Bible teacher Reuben Torrey so well expressed it:

> In the atoning death of His Son, instead of laying the punishment of guilty man upon an innocent third person, God took the shame and suffering due to man upon Himself; and so far from that being unjust and cruel, it is amazing grace![3]

At one time in my life I had to face two questions: Did Jesus die for me? And if He did, why did He? Since Sunday school days I had admired Jesus, but only recently had such questions begun to press me.

While in uniform during World War II I picked up a devotional booklet written by a fellow Jewish army chaplain. He was explaining the Passover to Jewish troops, and he used words like these: "You will discover in life that the innocent must suffer for the guilty. Such is the way to peace. But instead of it being all wrong, it is the answer to everything. The secret of life is sacrifice." To illustrate, he pointed to the young troops who did not create international quarrels but were being sent into combat to settle them. "To understand that," he said, "is to know the deeper meaning of existence."

I thought of Jesus. He was innocent, yet He was said to have suffered and died for the guilty. I felt this chaplain was on the track of something. I was a sinner. Jesus went to the cross, the innocent for the guilty—or so they said. It was, it seemed, the only way my sins could be forgiven. But did that mean Jesus actually took my place, that there had been a substitution?

It was evident there were some things I could not do for myself. I have never forgotten an occasion in the Aleutian Islands when two soldiers went to our commanding officer without my knowledge to defend their chaplain's actions. I was in trouble and could not defend myself. They went on my behalf and took my place to urge the bringing about of my vindication. Their kindness lingers in my memory as a sweet fragrance.

I was willing to grant that perhaps in some symbolic way Jesus died on my behalf, that He saw His role as that of a Messiah who would lay down His life for others in a kind of vicarious sacrifice.

What I couldn't see was why He would do it for me. In fact, I couldn't fathom why Jesus or anyone else would want to die for me. I told myself I was quite ready to take the rap for my shortcomings. I preferred to settle my own accounts, thank you very much.

A few years later a remarkable book made its appearance. It was a commentary on the Gospel of John by Arthur John Gossip, a Scottish preacher whom I had once heard and whom I deeply respected. I had read his other books and reveled in his wide learning and eloquent prose. I considered him a worthy man of God.

As I read Dr. Gossip's exposition of the Gospel of John, the old questions came back, still haunting me: *Did Jesus die for me?*

And if He did, why did He? I had reached the eighteenth chapter of the Gospel, which tells of Pilate's offer to release Jesus, since one prisoner was customarily set free at the Passover season. The crowd responded that they preferred the release of another prisoner named Barabbas, rather than Jesus.

At this point Dr. Gossip observed:

> With reason and truth scholars keep pointing out that when the New Testament Scriptures tell us that Christ died for us, the Greek preposition used means "on behalf of," and not "in the place of." For Barabbas at least there was no such distinction. And it is never clean cut. "On behalf of" keeps merging into "in the place of," do what you will.

Dr. Gossip then paid tribute to the British army troops with whom he served in France during World War I, saying that—

> those who laid down their lives there did it for us, on our behalf. That, certainly. That undeniably. But many feel that even that is an inadequate account of what they did and what we owe them, that they bore and died not merely upon our behalf but literally in our stead.

In conclusion, Gossip quoted Dr. James Denney, another noted Scottish theologian of the early twentieth century:

> What then is it which we are spared or saved from by the death of Jesus? What is it we do not experience because he died? The answer is that He saves us from dying in our sins. But for His death, we should have died in our sins; we should have passed into the blackness of darkness with the condemnation of God abiding on us. It is because He died for us, and for no other reason, that the darkness has passed away, and a light shines in which we have peace with God, and rejoice in hope of His glory.[4]

Since I read those words I have never again had problems with what theologians call the "substitutionary atonement of

Jesus Christ." The Holy Spirit has swept all my doubts off the lee side of the deck and they have never blown back. I believe that Jesus Christ took my sins upon Himself and died for me because He loved me and wanted me to be in heaven with Him. When I hear a preacher say, "God said it, Christ did it, I believe it, that settles it," I now add, "Amen. Hallelujah!"

That answer, however, does not take care of the question asked earlier in this chapter: Where do we get the joy? If it be true that we cannot have the joy without the salvation, it seems to be equally true that many Christians who have the salvation have missed out to a large extent on the joy.

So how do we get it?

The answer of Scripture is that joy is a fruit of the Holy Spirit. Fruit comes from abiding in the Vine, and Jesus is the Vine. When the fruit is ripe it is plucked, but we don't grow it, God grows it; and we don't pluck it, others do. As John implies, we pass on the joy and share it.

Thus joy is not something we *do*, but something we *receive* and to which we *respond*. It is a gift of grace through the Holy Spirit. And what is grace? It is unmerited favor from the hand of God, without any effort on our side—unearned, undeserved, and often unexpected. It is something that comes by the Holy Spirit without our initiating it, or causing it, or even fully understanding it. And the joy of our salvation is something that comes by grace.

The grace of God is like the sunshine; we didn't put it there, but we accept it thankfully, bask in it, use it, flourish and glory in it. Joy is something God wraps up in the gift of His grace. Actually it's everywhere. It is in the eye of a child, the trill of a meadowlark, the flight of a crane, the smile of a sleeping infant, the twinkle in the eye of a grandparent, the touch of a lover, the somersaults of a sea otter, the opening bars of the "Moonlight Sonata," the hug of a lost teenager who has come home—

> . . . a sunset touch,
> A fancy from a flower bell . . .
> A chorus-ending from Euripides . . . [5]

and the passing of one of God's beloved into the holy Presence.

Joy is there for the taking, and if you wish to grasp it, open your Bible to the hundredth Psalm and start to read. May the amazing grace of our Lord Jesus Christ and the touch of His ineffable joy be upon your spirit as you read and believe.

TWENTY-THREE

Take It All!

Take joy, my King, in what You hear;
Let it be a sweet, sweet sound in Your ear.

—Laurie Klein

∽

JESUS HAD JUST COMPLETED A preaching tour of Galilee, and word of His ministry was spreading like a California brushfire. When He returned to Capernaum on the north shore of the lake, He found the crowds larger than ever. Calling out His disciples, He took them with Him up the steep hillside to a favorite spot, seated Himself, and began to teach them. What came forth was a superb message of joy known as the Sermon on the Mount.[1] Today it comes to us out of the past, a remarkable transmission of eternal truth.

When we open our New Testament to the beatitudes in Matthew 5 we find that the first word Jesus spoke was "blessed" or, as it is in Greek, *makarios*. The ancient Hebrew meaning of the word was "favor from God." Whatever the language, whether Hebrew, Greek, or English, it is a great word, a magnificent word, yesterday, today, and forever. Here is what Dr. William Barclay has to say about *makarios*:

> The blessedness which belongs to the Christian is not a blessedness which is postponed to some future

world of glory; it is a blessedness which exists here and now. It is not something into which the Christian will enter, it is something into which he (or she) has entered. It is a present reality to be enjoyed. The Beatitudes say in effect, "O the bliss of being a Christian! O the sheer happiness of knowing Jesus Christ as Master, Savior and Lord!" The very form of the Beatitudes is the statement of the joyous thrill and the radiant gladness of the Christian life. In face of the Beatitudes a gloom-encompassed Christianity is unthinkable.

Makarios then describes that joy which has its secret within itself, that joy which is serene and untouchable and selfcontained, that joy which is completely independent of all the chances and changes of life. The Beatitudes speak of that joy which seeks us through our pain, that joy which sorrow and loss, pain and grief are powerless to touch, that joy which shines through tears, and which nothing in life or death can take away.

The world can win its joys and the world can equally well lose its joys. But the Christian has the joy which comes from walking forever in the company and in the presence of Jesus Christ. The Beatitudes are triumphant shouts of bliss for a permanent joy that nothing in the world can ever take away.[2]

Yet sadly today the word "blessing" no longer carries the same significance it had in the ancient world of commerce in Bible times, or even in the last century. It has been relegated to the religious vocabulary. Ask any bartender what a "blessing" is and he may reply, "A bit of luck." Many preachers have substituted the word "happy" for "blessed" in the hopes that their meaning will be understood. That hasn't worked very well either.

For example, the first beatitude Jesus taught was "Blessed are the poor in spirit, for theirs is the kingdom of heaven." To change that to "Happy are the poor in spirit" is to create a contradiction. Whatever else the spiritually poor may be, they are probably not happy. Even more inept is the second beatitude: "Happy are those who mourn." It makes very little sense to describe mourners as being happy people while they are mourning, particularly when that is not what Jesus meant.

What English word, then, can properly clarify and convey Jesus' meaning? In this connection Gerhard Kittel's *Theological Dictionary of the New Testament* contains an interesting statement by Professor Friedrich Hauck of Erlangen, Germany. I quote from Dr. Geoffrey Bromiley's translation: "The special feature of the term *makarios* [blessed] in the New Testament is that it refers overwhelmingly to the distinctive joy which accrues to man from his share in the salvation of the Kingdom of God."[3]

That's it! What Jesus was talking about was a deep "distinctive joy" which He promised would come to those who chose to partake, as Dr. Hauck said, in the "salvation of the Kingdom of God."

Let's see how the beatitudes would sound with such wording:

> Let the poor in spirit take joy, for theirs is the kingdom of heaven.
> Let those who mourn take joy, for they shall be comforted.
> Let the meek take joy, for they shall inherit the earth.
> Let those who hunger and thirst after righteousness take joy, for they shall be filled.
> Let the merciful take joy, for they shall obtain mercy.
> Let the pure in heart take joy, for they shall see God.
> Let the peacemakers take joy, for they shall be called children of God.
> Let those who are persecuted for righteousness' sake take joy, for theirs is the kingdom of heaven.

You will note that the beatitudes suddenly become not descriptions of the present, but promises for the future. Not acquisition, but hope. Not endurance, but relief. Not a reward for spiritual achievement, but a joyous outpouring of the love of God into the hearts of believers by the Holy Spirit.

How then does this fresh rendering of the beatitudes relate to people who are under enormous pressure, who are facing troubles that seem insurmountable? How do they relate to the crushed Christian wife whose husband has just informed her that he is leaving her? To the downcast teenage youth who has been dropped from the athletic squad for an infraction, just after he was elected team captain?

Let's examine the text.

"Let the poor in spirit take joy, for theirs is the kingdom of heaven." The late Dr. Harold Ockenga once explained, "In order to be filled with the Spirit we must meet God's conditions. To begin with, we confess to God that we are *not* filled with the Spirit."[4] "Poor in spirit" could mean a sense of failure, self-pity, depression, hopelessness, lack of faith, or lack of self-confidence. Jesus knew what He was talking about. To be emptied of negative spirits is exactly what we need before we can receive a fresh filling of the Holy Spirit. We go to the cross, we are crucified with Christ, and then—we take joy!

The reason so many earnest, sincere believers are failing to find joy in their Christian life is that they are not filled with the Spirit. And the reason they are not filled with the Holy Spirit is that they are occupied with all the unholy spirits—that is to say, the critical attitudes—and these spirits monopolize the believers' time and effort: hostility, resentment, fear, bitterness, envy, revenge, antagonism, arrogance, self-love . . . the list goes on and on. To be filled with the Spirit is to be filled with love. How can one enjoy the fullness of the Holy Spirit, who is God, when one is filled with everything else?

"Let those who mourn take joy, for they shall be comforted." The response of mourning is God's natural provision for meeting the tragedies of life. Tears are God's healing balm in times of grief. God never designed the stiff upper lip. He made us flexible to meet the demands of life. Eventually the mourning season will end, and the pain will subside. There is a balm in

Gilead. God will send comfort and restoration and the joy will come back.

"Let the meek take joy, for they shall inherit the earth." Meekness is always being misconstrued as timidity, which is preposterous. When a soldier or sailor salutes his superior, is that being timid? Consider the illustration of a shut door. Three persons wish to go through it. One is aggressive, and he kicks the door down because he thinks it is locked. Another stands in front of it timidly, afraid to test whether it is locked or not. A third person is meek. He tests the door to see whether it is unlocked. If it is, he opens it and walks through. Christians are not aggressive or timid; they are meek.

"Let those who hunger and thirst for righteousness' sake take joy, for they shall be filled." To make the right choice and feel the joy of it is one of life's greatest thrills. I heard one young man say in church, "I have changed my address, folks. I used to live on Broadway, but I've moved over onto Straight street. If you want to talk, that's where you'll find me."[5] To get on track we have to realize there is a right way and a wrong way. Choose the right, hunger and thirst for righteousness before God, and God will fill you with His Spirit and with joy.

"Let the merciful take joy, for they shall obtain mercy." Jesus is not talking about deals or bargains: "Do this and I'll give you that." To make a bargain with God one must have something to bargain with, and if we had anything to bargain with we wouldn't need mercy. Repentance is no help, for it is the liquidation of all helps. God exercises crown rights over what is His own, but He wants people to go to the cross so He can pour His mercy into them, make them merciful, and fill them with joy.

"Let the pure in heart take joy, for they shall see God." Purity of heart is not common. We Christians think we have our temptations under control, but they keep resurfacing. The world knows it, and God knows it. What must we look like to God? We are all unprofitable servants, but there is a daily recourse:

> I must needs go home by the way of the Cross,
> There's no other way but this.[6]

The Bible tells us, "If we confess our sins, He is faithful and just to forgive us our sins and to cleanse us from all unrighteousness" (1 John 1:9). So take joy! From joy comes purity of heart. Jesus knew: He was also tempted.

"Let the peacemakers take joy, for they shall be called sons of God." Once in Scotland I stopped two young lads who were fighting furiously in an Edinburgh street. I asked them whether they would quit if I offered each a penny. (Pennies in those days were large coppers.) The boys agreed; they shook hands and fell into each other's arms, then went off laughing to spend their lucre. But bribes will not bring a cease-fire today; the rancor runs too deep. God is the only Peacemaker. Our message is that our Father sent His Son, Jesus Christ, to make peace through the blood of the cross. Martial arts will never achieve peace. Jesus Christ will, and He will add to it the Joy of the Lord.

"Let those who are persecuted for righteousness' sake take joy, for theirs is the kingdom of heaven." Madame Jeanne Marie Guyon wrote, "When once we have enjoyed God and the sweetness of His love, we shall find it impossible to relish anything but Himself."[7] Madame Guyon spent 30 years in confinement for her faith, a victim of persecution by her own church. Eight of those years were spent in the notorious Bastille in Paris. For a persecuted Christian to take the joy of the Lord into the dungeons of this world is, from the human standpoint, impossible; but with God all things are possible.

Particularly interesting are the next two verses, which have more to say about persecution "for righteousness' sake." In this rendering they say, "Take joy when men revile you and persecute you and say all kinds of evil against you falsely for my sake. Be joyful and exult with gladness, for great is your reward in heaven, for in the same way they persecuted the prophets who were before you."

Even before His ministry began, according to the Gospel of Mark, Jesus was encountering stiff opposition. His adversary was Satan, whom He met in the desert, and overcame with three passages from the Old Testament. Shortly afterward Jesus returned to Galilee and healed a paralyzed man, telling him his sins were forgiven. Jesus thereby raised up some human persecution, which increased after He ate a meal with some questionable characters and performed a healing on the Sabbath. By the beginning of the third chapter of Mark, Jesus' enemies were plotting to get rid of Him.

From our frontier days comes a saying that when you are up to your neck in alligators, it's hard to keep your mind on the fact that you're there to drain the swamp. When people are following you, hounding you, and trying to entrap you, it's hard to maintain a serene countenance of joy. And when you are trying to clear commercial vendors out of a holy sanctuary, it's hard to exude a spirit of goodwill.

Over the next three years the "keepers of the law" sought to turn the Man of Joy into a Man of Sorrows. There is a sense no doubt in which the title "Man of Sorrows" properly and appropriately applies to Jesus. It is a messianic title, and Jesus in fulfilling His Father's will unquestionably assumed the prophetic role so movingly described in Isaiah 53.

Yet when Christians speak of Jesus as a "Man of Sorrows" who was "acquainted with grief," they are not describing His inner spiritual nature. Grief was sometimes flung at our Lord by His enemies with floggings and curses. He did not exchange His joy for sorrow; the sorrow came entirely from without, but the joy remained within. If Jesus became acquainted with grief, it was only to endure it.

Perhaps it has occurred to you to question why the artistic figure of our Savior is so seldom depicted with a benign or joyful expression on His face. Traditionally He appears in a state of extreme agony. It should be remembered that as horrible as the crucifixion was, and as momentous for our salvation as it proved to be, it was followed by the resurrection, in which the Heavenly Father turned death and despair into glorious victory. That victory is still being celebrated by followers of The Way, not only at the Easter season but every day of the calendar year.

Jack Jewell's painting of Jesus, "The Risen Christ by the Sea," is a serious attempt to put a genuine expression of joy on the face of Jesus. Naturally, Christians are divided in their reaction to the smile. But if Jesus' hearty expression says anything to me, it says frankly, "Take joy." It says, "Exult. Shout. Leap. Dance. Laugh. Away with long-faced sobriety, with false reverence and manufactured intensity in dealing with sacred matters."

I know that in some churches today the message is "Give. Give, and the Lord will bless you. Give, and we will make our budget." In the beatitudes the word of Jesus is rather "Take." It is a prophetic word: "Take, take, take the joy now, for the future is my Father's and the future is yours."

TWENTY-FOUR

The Joy-Filled Church

Joseph did whistle and Mary did sing,
Mary did sing, Mary did sing,
And all the bells on earth did ring
For joy our Lord was born.

—ANONYMOUS

THE CHURCH OF JESUS CHRIST is the most exciting, the most spectacular, the most beautiful body of good people in the world. If you are a Christian, these are your people. For two millennia these "saints" have been "marching" and "turning the world upside down," and now they are entering their third millennium.

The Christian community was founded by Jesus Christ Himself. The New Testament church was a church militant, and it still is the church militant, while on its way to becoming the church triumphant in the kingdom of God. Today it is "as visible and as bodily," says Reginald Fuller, "as the individual Christian."

Each time a new congregation is formed in prayer and seeks and receives the blessing of God, that new band of believers becomes a part of the church universal. As you probably already know, it is not unusual for one part of the church to claim to be "the only true church." We need not be unsettled by such claims. Jesus is the Head of the church, His Holy Spirit runs the church, and the Spirit is as free as the wind. No one individual and no church has ever captured, boxed, commandeered, or expropriated the Holy Spirit, but He knows those who are His.

Jesus has given His church a joyful message. It is the greatest news that ever came to the human race. No other system of belief in the world can match the Gospel of Christ in its glad assurance of God's love and His provision for our salvation.

If you want joy, find a church where there are some merry Christians—not cultists but ordinary, genuine, down-home Christians—and join them in their fun. Find some pastor whose prayer life results Sunday after Sunday in true Bible preaching; who will feed your soul with a Gospel sermon out of the Book and leave you wishing for more; and whose real life matches his ministry.

Sunday churchgoing can be a magnificent adventure. To see a congregation rise up and cheer a straightforward proclamation of truth is joy at its most exalted. To watch people of all ages respond to an invitation to receive Jesus Christ as Savior and Lord, after a presentation of the faith once delivered to the saints, is a thrilling and blessed experience.

But there is more to joy in church than just listening to superb rhetoric. Many paths of ministry are open to Christians who are willing and able to respond. I'm not talking about ushering and singing, very important as they are. I'm talking now about the deep inner enjoyment that is open to believers who put on the garment of praise and start witnessing for Christ in the marketplace.

George Gallup, Jr., the well-known pollster, speaking at an urban ministries conference in New Jersey, revealed some unusual statistical data drawn from his recent polls concerning what he called the "high spiritual faith" of certain American Christians today. I quote:

> These people are a breed apart. They are more toler-
> ant of people of diverse backgrounds. They are more

involved in charitable activities and practical Christianity. They are absolutely committed to prayer. They are far, far happier than the rest of the population. These are the quiet saints in our society who have a disproportionate, powerful impact on our communities.[1]

In the light of such glowing reports, why is it that most churches in America have less than 100 members, and seem to have great struggles to meet their bills at the end of each month? These are splendid people, the salt of the earth. Their characters are sound. Their theology is orthodox. Their salvation is sure. Their ministers are dedicated and sincere. What is it that keeps the congregation from natural growth? What is making so many of their leaders confess their discouragement?

I don't know, but I have a notion. It is only a speculation, and I expect many will disagree with me. They could be right, but I still hold my notion. I think what is lacking in many churches is the joy of the Lord.

As I see it, the church as a whole has treasured all of this rich golden ore of the Gospel, but doesn't always seem to know how to refine it. Too often it presents the Gospel in what Milton called "a dimm religious light" that obscures the plain teaching of repentance and deliverance.[2] We make the way to Jesus seem too steep for the ordinary person. There are too many flights of stairs, too much religious blathering. We transmute the upbeat promises of joy, good cheer, and lightheartedness that are indigenous in the New Testament into something legalistic, heavy, and depressing. Even though people really like and admire Jesus, they don't feel good enough or strong enough to make the spiritual effort to follow Him (yet Jesus said, "My burden is light").

Let's look again at where we stand. The New Testament has given the church a clear understanding of the biggest problem facing the human race, which is simply how to face a holy God just as we are: sinners. The king, the queen, the president, the lawmaker, the lawbreaker, the bishop, the prostitute, the butcher, the baker, the candlestick-maker, and you and I have all come short of the glory of God. As we are, He cannot, should not, and will not receive us. We're not worthy of heaven. So who is?

The church holds the answer, and the answer is Jesus. He came and spanned the gulf between God and sin. The church can proclaim to the world that in Christ our "God problem" has been solved. Even though we are sinners, we can relax. By faith in Jesus we are justified before God. By faith we are washed in the blood of the Lamb. We can now face God in His holiness. The vicarious sacrifice for sin has been made. The Lamb of God has been slain, the price has been paid, the blood has been shed for our redemption. Our sins are absolved by the grace of God and our future is secure. Thanks to the work on the cross of our Lord Jesus Christ, the ticket to heaven is already filled out. The Holy Spirit has it waiting for us at the airport.

Wow! If that isn't good news, I don't know what is. Don't say to me, "Yes, but . . . " I'm not listening. I won't argue. No soul was ever saved by a "yes, but." No church ever blessed town or city with a message of "yes, but." There is no "yes, but" about our sins. They are real. The Gospel tells us what to do about them. Either the Gospel is true or it isn't. Either a church is preaching the Gospel or it isn't.

I love to think about a train, for I grew up in the age of trains. The church is a Gospel train, heading out from the depot for a straight run to heaven. It's a fun ride. It's a free ride if you have your ticket. It's a clean ride, a beautiful ride, a joyful ride. The devil despises the Gospel train and is intent on derailing it, but God has His church crew working on the railroad right-of-way. That train is going through. All we have to do is climb aboard, keep our seats, and don't lean out the window.

Samuel Porter Jones, one of the South's greatest preachers, had a classic way of inviting people into the kingdom of God who don't think they're ready for it. His humor drew huge crowds of people. His early life was sodden with drink, but the joy of his salvation was so exhilarating that it made him a preacher in demand everywhere.

Mr. Jones approached one man with an invitation to come to Jesus and the man told him, "No, sir, I ain't fitten."

Mr. Jones said to him, "Come up here and get 'fitten.'"

But the man replied, "I ain't fitten to get fitten."

Jones said, "Let me tell you that the very fact that you don't feel fit is the thing that commends you to God. I have never felt worthy of membership in the church of Jesus Christ."[3]

It is because the church is such a blessing to humanity, and because I was once nurtured in it and love it today more than ever, that I suggest that as the Gospel is proclaimed today there is often an omission in its message. For years I didn't see the omission, though I felt the lack. Dr. Lloyd John Ogilvie, the current honorable chaplain of the United States Senate, put his finger on it:

> Joy is the missing ingredient in contemporary Christianity. The problem is our powerless piousness and grim religiosity.

The missing ingredient! Jesus came bringing a message of joy to the world, and where has it gone? When will all the churches begin smiling and singing with fervor and loving each other, and otherwise behaving so that the world learns what it really means to know Jesus Christ? The Bible says there is a time to laugh and a time to dance. I would say that the time has come; we've had enough somber religious paintings, statues, and icons. We've had enough reprimands from strait-laced church officials about respecting their own dignity.

Tommaso Campanella (1568-1639), a Dominican monk who spent 26 years in a Naples prison for his political and religious views, wrote a sonnet, "On the Resurrection," that registered an early protest. Here it is, translated from the Italian:

> If Christ remained but six hours on the cross
> after a few years of sorrow and affliction,
> which He suffered willingly for humankind
> that Heaven might be purchased forever,
> why is He everywhere to be seen

painted and preached only in torments
which were light compared with the joy that followed
when the wicked world's cruel blows were finished?

Why not talk and write about the majestic Kingdom
He enjoys in Heaven and soon will bring to earth
to the glory and praise of His worthy Name?
O foolish crowd, because you are so earthbound
and have eyes only for the day of His ordeal,
you see His high triumph shorn of its true worth.[4]

People who talk about the need to take a less serious look at our common faith are often accused of levity. Yet I know of no sincere believer who wants to make jokes about the holiest things in life. That is the devil's work. Of course veneration and respect are always due to the Blessed Trinity. We are told to worship the Lord in the beauty of holiness; but that does not necessarily require the minor key. God told His prophet Isaiah, "I will . . . give them joy in my house of prayer."[5] Let's find it! The Psalms tell us to make a joyful noise to the Lord, to praise Him with all manner of instruments.

Some of the responsibility for the lack of joy in the church can be laid to the Bible translators. Over the centuries they have taken it upon themselves to render the original texts in subdued and "religious" language, which, while fairly accurate, nevertheless conceals some bright phrases and fresh, strong expressions in the Hebrew and Greek originals. For example, they will translate *spermologos* (seed-picking bird) as "babbler" and *skandalon* (offense, scandal) as "stumbling block."

When we examine the original manuscripts, we find that in small and subtle ways the hilarious atmosphere of Jesus and His followers has been quietly reduced in translation to something like sanctimony. John Ellington, translation consultant for the United Bible Societies, writes, "The Bible is replete with examples of [humor] that must have made the original readers smile or chuckle." He admits that "humor is notoriously difficult to translate," but adds that "many Bible translators are reluctant to convey humor even after it has been pointed out to them."[6]

Piety is not a wet blanket to extinguish joy. True piety *is* joy—spiritual joy, wonderful joy. Gladys Collins of Green Mountain, North Carolina, writes, "I am a member of a church. The area I live in is known as the Bible Belt. I believe you will find more churches here than anywhere in the world, yet when you attend a worship service in most places, you leave depressed. I believe we should leave joyful and full of the Holy Spirit." She is correct. Joy is probably the most underworked word in the Christian lexicon, yet the New Testament uses it lavishly.

So what are we church people really looking for? Why do we keep coming to church year after year? Is it to get religion? Or is it for spiritual insurance—we are fearful of something terrible happening? When I interviewed C.S. Lewis in Cambridge, England, in 1963 he told me, "I find it difficult to keep from laughing when I find people worrying about future destruction of some kind or other. Didn't they know they were going to die anyway? Apparently not."[7]

It is just possible that what we are looking for is that elusive, wonderful thing the Bible calls the Joy of the Lord. The truth is that joy has been an attribute of God ever since the beginning of creation. We have seen that in the book of Isaiah the Lord tells His prophet, "Be glad and rejoice forever in what I will create."[8] He uses two verbs, saying it twice for emphasis! Yet generation after generation of faithful believers have apparently been misled into thinking that joy does not exist in the Christian faith. Much of the problem is created not by our lack of awareness of the Divine Presence, but by the wholly unnecessary gravity with which our leadership protects its own dignity, and the unnatural churchly posturing that so easily passes into overbearing arrogance and conceit.

An Episcopal clergyman, Dudley Zuver, has observed, "One of the quickest and, on the whole, the most effective ways of getting rid of God is to reverence Him out of existence."[9] Add to the mix the seemingly endless protocol that ties our ecclesiastical proceedings into knots and proves an enormous waste of time, and we have the church of today.

Dorothy Sayers has pointed out that while "the Christian faith is the most exciting drama that ever staggered the imagination of man," we today have managed to "show the world the typical Christian in the likeness of a crashing and rather ill-natured bore—and this in the Name of One who assuredly never bored a soul in those thirty-three years during which He passed through the world like a flame."[10]

Where did we churchfolk lose out? How did we drift so far from the joy of the Lord? Does it not seem strange that we should be cut off—amputated—from the hope of the very thing that attracted us to church in the first place?

Some think it not at all strange. Either for theological or sociological reasons, they think Christians should spend their days sorrowing and weeping either over their own sins or the sins of the body politic. But the response of Hendrik Kraemer, the Dutch Christian leader whom the Nazis tortured in a concentration camp, was a passionate "NO!" In Edinburgh in 1951 I heard him say, "We Christians must get the joy of Christ back into our religion. We are denying Christ by losing it!" Elton Trueblood wrote in 1964, "The Christian is joyful, not because he is blind to injustice and suffering, but because he is convinced that these, in the light of the divine sovereignty, are never ultimate. The Christian can be sad, and often is perplexed, but he is never really worried, because he knows that the purpose of God is to bring all things in Heaven and on earth together under one head, even Christ."[11]

Finally, let us close with a quiet vow to do something to liven up our church. How? With a single word: evangelism! Here is the way William Tyndale, martyr and Bible translator, rendered that word so dear to our hearts in the prologue to his English translation of the New Testament, which was published in 1525:

> Evangelio (that we cal gospel) is a greke word, and signyfyth good, mery, glad and joyful tydings, that maketh a mannes hert glad, and maketh hym synge, daunce, and leepe for ioye.[12]

May God bless His church and fill it with "evangelio"!

Paradise Lost and Found

TWENTY-FIVE

Paradise Lost

What has happened to all your joy?

—GALATIANS 4:15 NIV

∽

YOU HAVE JUST FINISHED READING a rather rare book—a discussion of Christian joy by a Christian writer. For whatever good this book may contain, may the Great Giver of Joy receive the thanks and the glory at His altar of incense.

And now the hour of truth has arrived—for me. Until twenty-some years ago I felt a stranger to the joy of the Lord. Even during my years as a Christian, the cheerful face I put on often masked an ash-heap of discontent.

It's hard to know what to say about the dark side of my life before 1972. Rembrandt, a master of chiaroscuro, used dark shadow with superb artistry to accent the light colors of his paintings. My own darkness became so miserable that I dread to mention it. To do so in order that God may be glorified is not easy; yet it may help someone to learn that the Holy Spirit can turn a wormy soul into a swallowtail butterfly.

My problem had no relationship to the churches I served, or their members, or any people in the Christian organizations in which I worked. Generally I get along with people. Nor did it have anything to do with moral character as such, for I remained a good citizen and faithful husband and father—and still am.

But for many of my early years I held a grievance against the world, and probably would have held it against the living God if I had known Him—which I didn't. This grievance reflected my own deep inner sense of inadequacy, which was the real problem. I arrived on the planet as the last of six children, with an older brother who was taller, bigger, stronger, and faster than I, and who kept me pinned much of the time. At school I became "Little Squirt," a tail-ender, ignored on the playground and kept off the teams until I got the strange feeling that I wasn't even there.

"So what?" you ask. "What else is new? Lots of kids have problems adjusting at school."

Yes, but there was more. I resented being a cipher. Instead of a little-shot, grinding my teeth in frustration, I wanted to be a big shot running things. My blazing ambition, as the story-tellers used to say, knew no bounds but got me nowhere. This again was my own inadequacy expressing itself by contrast.

Upon reaching adolescence I began to spend sad moments before the mirror, despising myself in earnest, and refusing utterly to come to terms with my body. How I longed for a huge frame so I could wear school letters on my sweater in front of the girls and win accolades on the football field! I wanted better legs, longer arms, more height, a handsomer face. Instead I got nothing.

All this narcissism made me few friends, and since athletics were beyond my reach, I chose to be a writer. In a high school English class I came across this statement by Henry Thoreau: "The mass of men live lives of quiet desperation." That told me what the future would be like.

Berkeley High school was followed by the University of California across town. It did not take long for Philosophy 5-A, using the *De Rerum Natura* of Lucretius, to convince my soft-ened brain that Sunday school was poppycock and God did not exist. My parents were so informed.

One night when 17 years of age and still living at home, I couldn't sleep. I went into my father's study and found him sitting at his desk. (As a fund-raiser for relief causes he was away on long trips much of the time.) I said to him, "Dad, I don't like what I'm doing. I don't want to be a newspaperman. What I really want is to do something useful with my life, something that will help people; but I'm stuck. I don't know what to do."

My father, as I learned later, had been saved in a Methodist church meeting in Jamestown, North Dakota, at the age of 21. He must have spoken encouraging words to me that night, but I've forgotten what they were. I'm certain he did not mention the Name of Jesus. He sent me back to bed and life went on.

For some reason a fraternity chose to pledge me. As an under-classman I was forced to endure attempts at molestation by some big "brothers" during after-dinner roughhousing—"all in fun"—and I also learned how to fight like a tiger. Some other young men in that fraternity were, as I recall, good scholars and strong, outstanding Christians. I turned away from them and preferred to trail after the jazzy set which occupied its free time drinking, smoking, swearing, and singing ribald songs.

The fraternity leaders knew me to be a minister's son, and were not impressed by my blowhard efforts to become a BMOC (big man on campus). When they chose a chaplain for their housemeetings, they passed me by. Meanwhile I aimed at the editorship of *The Daily Californian* and missed it.

In the first seven years after graduation from college I worked as a reporter on newspapers in California, Hawaii, and Alaska. At age 29 I quit the profession. It was time to face the facts: I had failed as a writer, having completed two books, neither of which ever appeared in print. I had also stumbled at other things, being unmarried, unemployed and virtually penniless, while all my classmates were moving steadily up the ladder of economic success.

Religion never had been a vocational interest of mine, even though two of my brothers had become ministers. I had gradually returned to a belief in God, but He remained to me a kind of "oblong blur." It was at this point, having seemingly failed at everything else, that I yielded to my brothers' persuasion and in 1940 applied for admission to a theological seminary.

No spiritual "call" from God or anyone else affected this decision. There were no rapturous moments. A silent prayer was about all the spirituality I could muster. My situation probably resembled in some way that of Sinclair Lewis' *Elmer Gantry,* whose "call" to the ministry came while tossing off a few beers in a speakeasy bar. My former fraternity president set the stage by informing me, "Frankly, I can't fancy you in the pulpit."

It really was preposterous, and I laugh at it now. At the time I stood a country mile from the Lord, but didn't know that I didn't know Him. At the theological seminary in which I enrolled it didn't seem to matter much whether I did know Him or didn't. The weekly quizzes included questions such as "Why did Paul say that Hagar was Mount Sinai?" and "Would I discuss the metaphysics of individualistic personalism?"

Two encounters during seminary years penetrated my darkness. Pearl Harbor had brought America into World War II, and with my IV-D draft deferment I spent a summer working for the war effort at a Navy docksite in upper San Francisco Bay. As a time-checker it became my duty each morning and afternoon to contact visibly the construction crewmen on the job.

In doing so I met a pleasant, middle-aged ditchdigger named Steve. Someone told me that Steve professed to be a Pentecostal Christian, and as the docksite personnel were not particularly known for their spirituality, I was curious. Striking up a conversation with Steve one day, I asked him if he went to church.

He leaned on his shovel and said, "Yes, I go to church. It's Wednesday, and I'll be there tonight."

"Do you enjoy church?" I asked.

"Well, yes, I enjoy the Word," he responded. "Sometimes I get real hungry for it, like I do for a piece of beefsteak."

A piece of beefsteak? The Bible?

Some weeks later I met another man while hitchhiking from my seminary in Berkeley to the Navy dock. This gentleman was driving an old Model-A Ford and stopped to pick me up. After shaking hands with me he smiled, and asked me if I were saved.

I hated it when people asked me that. (Now I love it.) I simply didn't know whether I was saved or not. I told him I was a theological student. That not being quite the answer he wanted, for the next few miles I listened to the warmest, most enthusiastic tribute to the love and the power of Jesus Christ that I have ever heard. I kept thinking, "He's not a minister. He has nothing to gain from this. Why is he doing it?"

Graciously, the man did not pursue questioning me. He simply exuded the joy of the Lord's salvation. It so poured out of his heart that it left me wondering, What am I missing in my Christianity? At a highway crossing he dropped me off with another handshake, then smiled and wished me the best.

I never forgot either of those men.

Two years earlier I had married a godly Christian girl who really knew the Lord. She and her equally godly mother had original-version Scofield Bibles. It took time, but eventually they led me to faith in Christ, and the spiritual change became very real. They had the Holy Spirit. They simply ignored what I was being taught in seminary and fed me with the "beefsteak" of God's Word. They taught me to stop preaching *about* the Bible and start preaching *the* Bible. I finished seminary, served 26 months as chaplain (captain) in the Army Air Corps, earned a doctorate of philosophy in Scotland on the subsidy of the "GI Bill of Rights," came back to the San Francisco area, and pastored churches for eight years until 1959.

By this time I was able to preach a salvation message, and the people appreciated it. Yet the devil continued to make me feel as if life had cheated me, and I often wondered, Why couldn't I have been somebody else? This nagging, discontented atmosphere even affected relationships with my family. Theologically I was bound for heaven, but actually I still held on to the unhappiness of who I was, and drenched my soul in self-pity. I read books, took graduate courses, sat in lectures at the Jung Institute in Switzerland, became a patient in a Scottish psychotherapy clinic, and even tried to study logic. I continually sought to find out what was wrong with me. I learned at last the problem, and should have known it from childhood: I simply didn't like myself.

In April 1958 Billy Graham came to San Francisco for a seven-week crusade. I had arrived at being a confirmed, praying evangelical, and liked both Billy and his message. Doors opened for me to write a book about his crusade, and Billy liked what I wrote. Thanks to him and his teammates, my first book was published by Harper as *Crusade at the Golden Gate*. In December of that year Billy telephoned one night, inviting me to join his team and to become editor of a new magazine he was planning. I moved my family to Minneapolis, Minnesota, and lived there 17 years. *Decision* magazine became the largest Christian magazine in the world, with a monthly circulation of 5 million copies.

Yes, things were great, except that . . .

When Satan finds a weakness in a Christian, he wastes no time exploiting it. The psalmist speaks of becoming "a stranger and sojourner from God." Like Bunyan's Christian in *Pilgrim's Progress*, I was floundering in the Slough of Despond and finding it had no bottom. Externally I had become a successful Christian journalist; internally my soul hurt. One word expressed my deepest feeling: "fury." There were times when I even lost interest in living. For a Christian, this is an ugly matter.

After the book about Billy Graham's 1958 crusade appeared, my next literary effort fell flat.

Meanwhile I watched other merry Christians around me smiling, laughing, seeming to live cheerful lives under the blessing of the Holy Spirit. Gloom did not fill the Bible I read each day. Some of the churches I attended sang cheerful songs. The people I worked with had their own problems, but they kept them to themselves and put on a bright face. The news of the day sounded bad but no worse than usual. The problem was simply me, me, me. I could not relax and enjoy. The devil had succeeded in robbing me of that beautiful something the Bible calls the joy of the Lord. It seemed beyond my attainment.

TWENTY-SIX

Paradise Found

O joy too high for my low style to show!
O bliss fit for a nobler state than me!

—PHILIP SIDNEY

∾

SEATED AT MY EDITORIAL DESK at *Decision* magazine one day in 1971, I opened a letter from a much-admired friend, Leonard Ravenhill. This man had authored many powerful books, including *Why Revival Tarries*. He was writing from Nassau in the Bahamas, and his letter was dated December 2. Here is what it said:

> Dear Woody: When meetings last until after midnight; when couples tear up their divorce papers before a thousand people; when the chief of police says that there is a rash of confessing of crimes; when the shopkeepers say they are staggered by the great number of folk owning up to shoplifting; when lawyers, psychologists, and a Jesuit priest get saved; when deacons and many church members confess with tears and with great shame and brokenness that they have been living in adultery, fornication, thieving, and lying; when men from those meetings in Saskatoon, Canada, fly east to preach at the

199

Toronto Bible College chapel hour, and the hour lasts until one the next morning, with great humiliation and confessions—when all this and loads more happens night after night for several weeks, one might say that there is a touch of REVIVAL.

No star-studded platform, no huge budget, no gimmicks were in evidence. Indeed, the two evangelists had a bagful of modern tricks and they threw them all out and cast themselves upon the blessed Holy Spirit. Result: Right now the Canadian city of Saskatoon, Saskatchewan, is shaking under the power of God. The outbreak is city-wide.

Hop a plane, my brother, and get a "foretaste of glory divine!" This is a prelude to the next great manifestation of God. Hallelujah to the Lamb! Praying for you always,

—Leonard Ravenhill

Earlier I had read something about that Canadian revival in the Saskatoon press. The report said specifically that the large Simpson-Sears store in the city had to open a special account to take care of all the "conscience money" being returned by shoplifters who had been revived at meetings in the local Baptist church. (To Christians who seriously want to know the difference between enthusiastic evangelistic meetings and the direct heavenly touch of the Holy Spirit, I suggest a test of conscience might help—such as shoplifting being paid for.)

In response to Len's letter, I decided this might indeed be a story for *Decision* magazine, and accordingly I telephoned the Saskatoon church. I was told that the "revival" had moved. The American evangelists, Ralph and Lou Sutera, were ministering in Regina, and the Saskatoon pastor, Rev. Wilbert McLeod, was conducting meetings nightly in Elim Chapel, Winnipeg.

I then telephoned Gertrude Adrian, the Billy Graham team's Canadian office manager, and asked her, "Is it true a revival is happening there in Winnipeg?"

Her reply was, "That's funny. I was revived last night."

On Wednesday, December 15, 1971, I flew to Winnipeg, took a room in a hotel, and attended the evening service in Elim Chapel. Hundreds of people, mostly young, had filled the place and were singing some unfamiliar choruses and joyous spiritual songs. The whole evening, except for a brief talk, consisted of warm, enthusiastic singing, praying, some laughter, and many testimonies. I had never seen or heard anything like it. No invitation was ever given, but before the close of the minister's brief message more than a hundred young and old inquirers spontaneously crowded the area in front of the pulpit and clambered around the chancel, seeking something called revival.

Later an "afterglow" took place at a nearby church and nearly everyone in Elim Chapel (except for the inquirers) trooped over in zero weather. I joined them and heard more testimonies and requests for prayer. It went on until the wee hours of the morning. The next day I flew back to Minneapolis, awed and troubled, my head full of what I had seen and heard.

The speaker at the Winnipeg service was the Reverend Wilbert McLeod. Formerly a Shantyman preacher on Vancouver Island, he now pastored Ebenezer Baptist Church in Saskatoon. The touch of the Holy Spirit had occurred in his church. Preaching that night from the third chapter of Paul's letter to the Colossians, Mr. McLeod said some things that burned into my memory. Among them:

"The Holy Spirit is love. To be filled with the Spirit is to be filled with love.

"You can't change anybody, but God can change you.

"The church has been sweeping things under the rug. God is pulling back the rug.

"Revival is nothing but the Holy Spirit pointing His finger right at you.

"If you wish to be filled with the Spirit, you must deal with your problem." (*How did he know I had a problem? Some problem!*) "Go to your knees and deal with it in prayer. While you are doing that, ask God to put you on the cross and crucify you." (He quoted Galatians 2:20.) "After you have been spiritually crucified with your Lord, you can pray to be filled with His Holy Spirit. You can even thank God in advance for doing it."

Here were some of the revival testimonies I heard that night: "I feel as if God's steamroller had just run over me" . . . "When God uses a solvent He does a good job" . . . "This is group therapy with Christ as the focal point" . . . "Any old bush will do as long as it is on fire!" . . . "People who are right with God can help each other" . . . "If you are not ready to deal with your sin, perhaps you had better go home and 'pickle' awhile" . . . "I feel as if a 200-bag of flour has been lifted from my back, but on the way to the meeting I prayed for a flat tire so I wouldn't have to go" . . . "Crucifying the self is a painful experience but it's the only way to the blessing."

Some of my pastor friends in the Twin Cities knew I had visited the Winnipeg revival, and were curious to learn what I heard and saw. They expressed to me an interest in bringing some of the people involved in it to speak in their churches. A month later two laypeople who had been touched, a bridge engineer and his wife, flew down for a weekend. I made the arrangements, and on Sunday, January 9, Harry and Evelyn Thiessen spoke in four Minnesota churches, often in tears. Their testimony was received with warmth and amazement.

That night after the last service, we arranged an afterglow in the basement of one Minneapolis church, similar to the one I had visited in Winnipeg. Perhaps 25 people stayed for it. It started out as one of those dreadful gatherings—a prayer meeting in which no one wants to pray. I felt responsible for the disappointment since I had invited our Canadian friends, and so decided to "prime the pump" by asking for prayer for myself. The Thiessens invited me to kneel at a chair in the middle of the room, and some people gathered around, laid hands on me, and prayed for me. Then I was told to pray.

What I didn't expect was that God would turn on the spigot. Once started, I did what I had never intended to do— spilled out my disappointment with life and my bitterness toward people who had contributed to my discontent. The Thiessens then told me to ask God to "crucify me," and then to ask God to fill me with His Holy Spirit. To be candid, since several people had their hands on me, there wasn't much else I could do.

Suddenly things became very intense and earnest for me. "The way of the cross" and "dying to self," for a person who thinks of himself or herself as a Christian, are not just expressions found in a hymnbook. Crucifixion is a holy business, touched by eternity. It means more than coming to the cross, being near the cross, yielding at the cross, laying down burdens at the foot of the cross, bearing the cross, or taking up the cross. Self-crucifixion means we have to be *nailed* to the cross! And since self cannot and will not slay self, it has to be done by faith. It meant my being led back to Calvary by the Spirit of God. I had to be wiped out spiritually until reckoned by myself as dead by faith.

I felt the fear of God and the terror of the Lord.

Once I was back on my feet, Evelyn Thiessen said to me, "You didn't feel anything, did you?" What could I say? I said nothing. Superficially I felt a bit humiliated and was also annoyed at the behavior of the others present, for it irritated me to think I had to be first. Evelyn smiled. "The feeling will come later," she said, "and how!"

Four or five days after Evelyn Thiessen had uttered those words "And how!" at the afterglow I was sitting quietly in a living room chair at home when I suddenly realized to my astonishment that I had no more animosity toward anyone. It was absolutely incredible. Pascal's famous description of his own experience of rapture came to me: "Joy, joy, joy, tears of joy!"

I asked myself, What had happened? Thinking back, the afterglow meeting on the previous Sunday came to mind. Could it be that? But I had sat through many prayer meetings. Then I realized with a shock Bill McLeod's words, "If you want to be filled with the Spirit . . . !" The Spirit of God! He was there! I remembered about the cross, and something evangelist Sam P. Jones once said came to my mind: "The Lord fishes on the bottom." I remembered, too, that when Dr. Will Houghton was asked how much a certain wealthy gentleman, now deceased, had left in his will, Dr. Houghton replied, "He left it all."

I wanted to laugh. Quietly, unmistakably, the Spirit of God had touched me. No sparks. No blue flame. But no longer was I unhappy with myself; in fact, I wouldn't be anyone else ever again! Everything I ever resented in life had vanished, like the Cheshire cat in the tree in *Alice in Wonderland*. All that was left was the smile! The truth was that nothing whatever in my situation or my relationships had changed, but bitterness and anger were now turned to thankfulness, leaving me with a wonderful feeling of peace and joy. I loved everybody.

Sitting there, making the first of many hesitant apologies to my wife for many things, I flipped open my Bible to one of my favorite passages, Nehemiah 8:10: "Go your way, eat the fat, drink the sweet, and send portions to those for whom nothing is prepared; for this day is holy to our LORD. Do not sorrow, for the joy of the LORD is your strength."

Two laymen friends had also asked for prayer that Sunday night and had hands laid on them. They too had been revived, and when I telephoned them they enthusiastically echoed my feelings. On the next Sunday evening I had a preaching engagement in Duluth, 160 miles away, and they agreed to accompany me through the snow. What a magnificent journey of joy! We couldn't stop talking! The evening at the church was equally enthusiastic, and people responded; at the end they asked for an "afterglow." A week later we were back.

The Holy Spirit was at work. The dark night was over. The joybells have never stopped ringing. I have seen and taken part in revival "afterglows" in Minnesota, Iowa, Wisconsin, South Dakota, California, Texas, Mississippi, Arizona, Alaska—well, God knows; I have forgotten, but the blessings go on.

Two things I have learned in the years since retiring and returning home to California for good. One is that the joy of the Lord is such a vast spiritual reality that no human mind can comprehend it. To borrow a phrase of Augustine, it "crams the heavens and the earth to overflowing," and all I have of it is a tiny thimbleful. But what a delight it is!

A second thing I have learned is that joy plays only a part in the Christian life, and not the most important part. The purpose and intent of the Bible is not to bring us joy, but to save our souls and fit us for God.

In these pages I have tried to be honest and open with you, as the apostles were with their fellows. Now let me say this as humbly and lovingly as I know how: Some of you reading this book really need to be born again. You're in no shape to meet with God, and you know it. Among my Christian readers, some of you would do well to ask, as I did, to be crucified with Christ, in order that the risen Christ might be formed in your hearts.

Unfortunately our environment in the new millennium will be full of traps. You need to be set free from the world just as the whale "J.J." was revived and set free from Sea World in San Diego, and returned to her beloved Pacific ocean. You need to return to your native habitat—the ocean of God's redeeming love. Apart from the Savior of the world, Jesus Christ, our struggle against evil is lost before we lift a hand. Tomorrow morning's newscast will tell you about it.

So our quest for joy closes on a modest note. We recognize that the Joy of the Lord follows a secondary course in the spreading of the Gospel of Jesus. Yet we spreaders need it so much every day! Why? Because of what it does for life. Edna St. Vincent Millay wrote some words that, taken out of context, seem to describe elegantly the truth about joy:

> . . . ah, my friends,
> and oh, my foes,
> it sheds a lovely light.

Note: If you write me in care of the publisher, I will see that you are introduced to authentic, genuine servants of Christ who will help you in your quest to find Jesus, Man of Joy.

—S.E.W.

NOTES

Foreword: "Bruce, I have one word . . ."

1. Psalm 8:2; Matthew 18:3,4

Introduction: The Phone Rang

1. *Jesus, Man of Joy* was first published by Here's Life publishers, San Bernardino, CA, in 1991, and was reissued by Thomas Nelson in 1992. That paperback edition is now out of print, but many of its chapters appear in this volume.
2. The "Matthew Film" address is Box 5068, Clifton, NJ 07015-5068.
3. Bruce Marchiano, *In the Footsteps of Jesus* (Eugene, OR: Harvest House Publishers, 1997).

Chapter 1: An Astonishing Change

1. Alfred Tennyson, "In Memoriam."
2. *San Francisco Chronicle*, July 13, 1990.

Chapter 2: Whose Idea Was This?

1. G.K. Chesterton, *Orthodoxy* (Garden City, NY: Doubleday, 1959), p. 160.
2. Luke 1:26ff.
3. Matthew 1:20,21.
4. Luke 1:46,47.
5. Luke 2:10.
6. Revelation 4:11 KJV.
7. Augustine's *Confessions*, Book X, 6.

Chapter 3: Where Did He Get It?

1. Hymn, "Praise, My Soul, the King of Heaven," 1834.
2. Luke 12:32.
3. Isaiah 65:18.
4. Zephaniah 3:17.
5. Joseph Addison, "Ode," in *The Spectator*, A.D. 1712.

Chapter 4: The Merry Jesus

1. The published English translation of the Lentulus document does not mention date or translator. The original Italian version is also in the Library of Congress.
2. Bruce Barton, *The Man Nobody Knows* (London: Constable, 1926), pp. 49-50.
3. Cf. Elton Trueblood, *The Humor of Christ* (San Francisco: Harper & Row, 1964); Cal Samra, *The Joyful Christ* (San Francisco: Harper & Row, 1985).
4. Matthew 9:15; 11:19; 12:3,4.
5. Michael K. MacIntosh, *The Tender Touch of God* (Eugene, OR: Harvest House, 1996), p. 200.
6. Billy Graham, *The Secret of Happiness* (Garden City, NY: Doubleday, 1955).
7. Luke 10:21.
8. See John 16:33.
9. John Knox, *The Man Christ Jesus* (Chicago: Willett & Clark, 1942), pp. 56-59.

Chapter 5: Uncommon Wedding

1. John 2:1-11.
2. Hebrews 1:9.
3. Isaiah 53:3.
4. Hebrews 12:2.
5. See John 2:3.
6. See John 2:5.
7. Walter Hooper, ed., "Miracles," in C.S. Lewis, *God in the Dock, Essays on Theology and Ethics* (Grand Rapids: Eerdmans, 1970), pp. 25-37. Originally a sermon preached at St. Jude on the Hill Church, London, November 26, 1942.
8. Matthew 14:16-20.
9. Matthew 12:10-13.
10. "Heureux les débonnaires, car ils heriteront de la terre."
11. Luke 6:38.
12. John 2:11.

Chapter 6: Religious Smog

1. In *Decision* magazine, October 1968.
2. Interview on May 7, 1963, published *inter alia* in Lewis, *God in the Dock*, p. 259.
3. Matthew 23:14.
4. Ed Wheat, M.D., *Love Life for Every Married Couple* (Grand Rapids: Zondervan, 1989), p. 12.
5. Samuel Chadwick, *The Way to Pentecost* (Fort Washington, PA: Christian Literature Crusade, 1976), pp. 35-36.
6. Acts 13:52.

Chapter 7: "Pecooler Noshuns"

1. Matthew 23:24; Mark 10:25; Luke 11:39; Matthew 12:26-28; Luke 6:39; Matthew 8:22; Luke 6:44; 8:16; Matthew 7:3-5.
2. Matthew 15:21-28.
3. William Barclay, *Daily Study Bible: The Gospel of Mark* (Edinburgh: Saint Andrew Press), p. 40.

4. *Topical Encyclopedia of Living Quotations* (Minneapolis: Bethany House, 1982), no. 1578.
5. Elton Trueblood, *The Humor of Christ* (San Francisco: Harper & Row, 1989).
6. Mark 1:16-20 NIV.
7. Mark 12:37.
8. *Topical Encyclopedia*, nos. 1139, 1137.
9. 2 Corinthians 4:7.

Chapter 8: Surfing the Scriptures

1. 2 Corinthians 5:19.
2. John 1:17.
3. Spurgeon's *Sermons* (London: Funk & Wagnalls, 1904), p. 34.
4. 1 John 1:8.
5. John Donne, "Hymn to God the Father."
6. Romans 3:22; Philippians 3:14.
7. Proverbs 15:13; 17:22; 15:23; Ecclesiastes 2:26; Romans 14:17.
8. Isaiah 61:1-3.
9. James S. Stewart, *River of Life* (Nashville, Abingdon Press, 1972).
10. John 3:16.

Chapter 9: Still Waters

1. From a free translation by Edward FitzGerald, published in 1859.
2. Psalm 31:16; 36:9; 67:1; 80:3; 80:7; 119:135.
3. Matthew 17:2.
4. Psalm 23:3.
5. Tennyson, *Idylls of the King*, The Coming of Arthur, line 500.
6. Zephaniah 3:17 NIV.

Chapter 10: Gold Without Tarnish

1. Taken from my account in *Decision* Magazine, March, 1973. At the close of the century both John and Ben Peterson are married, parents of five and four children respectively, and are active in full-time Christian service—John with Athletes in Action and Ben as assistant pastor of a Watertown, WI church.
2. See 1 Corinthians 9:24.
3. John 15:11.

Chapter 11: Will Moves Through Desire

1. Matthew 6:10 KJV.
2. Stephen Vincent Benét, "John Brown's Body," in *Selected Works*, vol. 1 (New York: Farrar & Rinehart, 1942), p. 187.
3. From a sermon preached by Dwight in Yale Chapel about 1799. Taken from *The World's Great Sermons*, vol. 3, Grenville Kleiser, comp. (New York: Funk & Wagnalls, 1908).
4. C.S. Lewis, *Surprised by Joy* (New York: Harcourt, Brace Publishers, 1956), p. 220.

Chapter 12: When God Shouts

1. Galatians 4:15 NIV.
2. Job 38:7.
3. Psalm 47:5.
4. Amos 3; Jeremiah 25:30 NIV; Ezekiel 43:2; 10:8; Exodus 3:4; Matthew 17:5; Revelation 6:1.
5. Matthew 3:1; Mark 9:7.
6. 1 Thessalonians 4:16.
7. Luke 15:10.
8. See Revelation 22:17.

Chapter 13: Silence Is Golden

1. P.T. Forsyth, *The Soul of Prayer* (London: Independent Press, 1954), pp. 13-14.
2. Sidney Lanier, *The Marshes of Glynn*.
3. Cf. "Ignatius to the Philadelphians," in *Ancient Christian Writers*, vol. 1, Epistles of St. Clement of Rome and St. Ignatius of Antioch, tr. J.A. Kleist (New York: Newman Press, 1946), p. 85.
4. C.F. Andrews, *Christ in the Silence* (London: Hodder & Stoughton, 1933), pp. 234-35.
5. Oliver Wendell Holmes, *The Music Grinders*.
6. Psalm 27:14.
7. Psalm 100.
8. Psalm 116. This psalm became known in World War II as the "Psalm of Bataan," as it was a favorite of American troops during the horrors of the "long march" following the fall of Corregidor in the early months of the war in the Pacific.
9. William Shakespeare, *King Lear*, Act 5, Scene 3.
10. 2 Corinthians 4:18.

Chapter 14: When Joy Meets Fear

1. Matthew 28:8.
2. Luke 24:41.
3. 1 John 4:18.
4. Adapted from Ephesians 6:13-17.

Chapter 15: Joy When It Hurts

1. Micah 6:8.
2. C.S. Lewis, *The Problem of Pain* (London: Geoffrey Bles, 1946), p. 98.
3. Frank Uttley, *The Supreme Physician* (London: James Clark & Co., n.d.).
4. Michael K. MacIntosh, *The Tender Touch of God* (Eugene, OR: Harvest House Publishers, 1996), p. 200.
5. Mark 5:25-29.
6. Lewis, *Problem of Pain*, p. 103.
7. Luke 13:16.
8. Habakkuk 3:17-19 NIV.
9. Psalm 51:8 NIV.

Chapter 16: What Is Happiness?

1. Aristotle's entire book should be read, particularly Book 4, Section 3. *The Nichomachean Ethics of Aristotle*, tr. D.P. Chase (London: J.M.Dent, 1949).
2. Blaise Pascal, *Pensées*, W.F. Trotter translation, Modern Library edition (New York: Random House, 1941, no. 425, Random House numbering).
3. William James, *The Varieties of Religious Experience* (New York: Penguin Books, 1958), p. 83.
4. Sigmund Freud, *Introductory Lectures on Psychoanalysis*, tr. Joan Riviere (London: George Allen & Unwin, 1949), pp. 298-99.
5. "Aristippus," article in *The Oxford Classical Dictionary* (Oxford: Clarendon Press, 1961), pp. 90-91.
6. Dostoevsky, *The Brothers Karamazov*, tr. Constance Garnett (New York: Modern Library, n.d.).

Chapter 17: God's Crepe Suzettes

1. 1 John 4:8.
2. Cf. Genesis 3:5.
3. Romans 14:17.
4. Luke 15:21.
5. Luke 15:24.
6. E.M. Forster, *A Passage to India*.
7. Numbers 14:18.
8. Francis Schaeffer, *Complete Works*, vol. 3 (Wheaton, IL: Crossway Books), p. 355.

Chapter 18: The Secret of Radiance

1. John 17:13 NIV.
2. Henry Alford, *The Greek New Testament*, fifth edition, vol. 1 (Grand Rapids: Baker Book House, 1980), pp. 177ff.
3. Arthur John Gossip, *The Galilean Accent* (Edinburgh: T. & T. Clark, 1927).
4. Alford, *New Testament*, p. 178.
5. Copies of Chuck Smith's many books may be obtained by writing to him at Word for Today Publishing Co., Box 8000, Costa Mesa, CA 92628.

Chapter 19: Joy and Overjoy

1. See Daniel 6:1-28.
2. Daniel 6:21.
3. Daniel 6:26-28.
4. Matthew 2:1-12.
5. Micah 5:2.
6. Matthew 2:10.
7. Luke 24:33,34.
8. Luke 24:36-43.
9. John 20:20 NIV.
10. Acts 12:1-19.
11. Acts 15:6ff.
12. Acts 12:19.

13. As a young girl in Michigan, Julia Wirt became the first woman telegrapher in the United States, endured gender harassment, and was befriended by a young fellow telegrapher named Thomas A. Edison, whose large autographed portrait she cherished.

Chapter 20: Faith Creating Joy

1. Romans 10:9.
2. Ephesians 2:8,9.
3. Cf. *A Theological Word Book of the Bible*, Alan Richardson, ed. (London: SCM Press, 1950), p. 75.
4. Hebrews 11:1.
5. Habakkuk 2:4.
6. *The Encyclopedia of Religious Quotations*, ed. Frank C. Mead (Westwood, NJ: Fleming Revell, 1965), p. 130.
7. Genesis 22:1-18.
8. Hebrews 11:33,38.
9. Matthew 18:20.
10. Matthew 11:30.
11. Psalm 37:1.
12. Matthew 6:25.
13. Luke 15:7.

Chapter 21: Hope That Brings Joy

1. 1 Corinthians 15:17,19 NIV.
2. Romans 1:4.
3. John S. Whale, *Christian Doctrine* (New York: Macmillan, 1942), p. 73.
4. Philippians 2:9; Colossians 1:17,18.
5. Acts 1:11.

Chapter 22: What's Amazing About Grace

1. John 10:18.
2. 2 Corinthians 5:19.
3. R.A. Torrey, *Questions Answered* (Chicago: Moody Press, 1909), p. 9.
4. A.J. Gossip, "Exposition of John," in *The Interpreter's Bible*, vol. 8 (Nashville: Abingdon Press, 1952), pp. 770-71.
5. Robert Browning, *Bishop Blougram's Apology*.

Chapter 23: Take It All!

1. Matthew 5-7.
2. William Barclay, *The Daily Study Bible: The Gospel of Matthew*, vol. 1 (Edinburgh: The Saint Andrew Press), pp. 83-85.
3. Gerhard Kittel and Gerhard Friedrich, *Theological Dictionary of the New Testament*, vol. IV, tr. G.W. Bromiley (Grand Rapids: Eerdmans, 1967), p. 367.
4. Harold J. Ockenga, in "The Third He," in *Decision* magazine, January 1969, p. 15.
5. A play on Acts 9:11.
6. Hymn, "The Way of the Cross Leads Home," by Charles H. Gabriel.
7. Mme. Guyon, "A Short and Very Easy Method of Prayer" (Philadelphia: George W. McCalla, 1925). Reprinted in *Spiritual Disciplines*, ed. S. Wirt (Westchester, IL: Crossway Books, 1983), p. 171.

Chapter 24: The Joy-Filled Church

1. From an address at a Southern Baptist conference in Newark, New Jersey, reported by Baptist Press and subsequently carried by the Evangelical News Service, May 24, 1991.
2. John Milton, *Il Penseroso.*
3. Samuel P. Jones, "Waiting and Hoping," in *Sermons and Sayings by the Rev. Sam P. Jones* (Nashville: Southern Methodist Publishing House, 1885).
4. Tommaso Campanella's sonnet "On the Resurrection" appeared in English translation in *Country of the Risen King,* an anthology of Christian poetry compiled by Merle Meeter (Grand Rapids: Baker Book House, 1978), p. 289.
5. Isaiah 56:7 NIV.
6. John Ellington, "Wit and Humor in the Bible," in *The Bible Translator* (New York: United Bible Societies, July 1991).
7. "Heaven, Earth and Outer Space," interview in *Decision* magazine, October 1963, p. 4.
8. Isaiah 65:18 NIV. In his brilliant study of Isaiah, Alec Motyer points out that "the doubling of the imperatives (take joy and exult) is itself a guarantee of total joy, as if saying it two ways encompassed every possible joyful feeling." See J.A. Motyer, *The Prophecy of Isaiah* (Downers Grove, IL: InterVarsity Press, 1993), p. 529.
9. Dudley Zuver, *Salvation by Laughter* (New York: Harper, 1933), p. 260.
10. Dorothy Sayers in *Topical Encyclopedia of Living Quotations* (Minneapolis, Bethany House, 1982), no. 261.
11. D. Elton Trueblood, *The Humor of Christ* (San Francisco: Harper & Row, 1989), p. 32.
12. William Tyndale (1494?–1536), evangelical scholar, was driven from England in 1524 and never returned. His first New Testament translation was forbidden in England but because of its vigor and other superb qualities it eventually became the basis of both the King James Bible and today's New King James Bible. Tyndale died as a martyr in Vilverde, Belgium, where he was arrested for defending the Gospel, condemned, tied to the stake, strangled by the hangman, and burned.

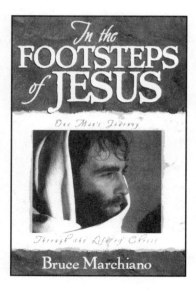

When actor Bruce Marchiano landed the role of Jesus in *The Gospel According to Matthew*, he knew God's hand had led him to this turning point. But he never imagined the lifechanging experiences that lay ahead.

Come with Bruce on this intensely personal journey as he walks in the footsteps of Jesus. You'll experience an intimate glimpse into the heart of God.

***Available from
your local bookstore***

Not a script about the Bible . . . *The Gospel According to Matthew* is the Bible on video, word for word from bestselling New International Version.

The four-tape series features actors Richard Kiley and Bruce Marchiano as Jesus. See the pages of the Bible come to life as this joyous portrayal of Jesus brings to the screen a divine yet warmly human Savior.

***See your local Christian retailer
or call 1-800-33-BIBLE
to order***